SCOTTISH HIGHLANDS

Contents

Using this Book

The entries in the Gazetteer have been carefully selected to reflect the interest and variety of the Scottish Highlands. For reasons of space, it has not been possible to include every community in the region. Certain towns, Aberdeen and Callander for example, which are not strictly within the Scottish Highlands, have been included because of their outstanding importance to the cultural and social life of the area as a whole.

Each entry in the A to Z Gazetteer has the atlas page number on which the place can be found and/or its National Grid reference included under the heading. An explanation of how to use the National Grid is given on page 80.

Beneath many of the entries in the Gazetteer are listed AA recommended hotels, guesthouses, garages and self-catering accommodation in the immediate vicinity of the place described. Hotels are also given an AA classification.

Please note: This guide lists only AA-appointed hotels selected for Special Merit Awards. For a full selection of AA-recommended hotels, please consult the AA guide, Hotels and Restaurants in Britain.

HOTELS

1-star	Good hotels and inns, generally of small scale and with good furnishings and facilities.
2-star	Hotels with a higher standard of accommodation. There should be 20% private bathrooms or showers.
3-star	Well-appointed hotels. Two thirds of the bedrooms should have private bathrooms or showers.
4-star	Exceptionally well-appointed hotels offering high standards of comfort and service. All bedrooms should have private bathrooms or showers.
5-star	Luxury hotels offering the highest international standards.

Hotels often satisfy *some* of the requirements for higher classifications than that awarded.

Red-star	Red stars denote hotels which are considered to be of outstanding merit within their classification.
Country House Hotel	A hotel where a relaxed informal atmosphere prevails. Some of the facilities may differ from those at urban hotels of the same classification.

GUESTHOUSES

These are different from, but not necessarily inferior to, AA-appointed hotels, and they offer an alternative for those who prefer inexpensive and not too elaborate accommodation. They all provide clean, comfortable accommodation in homely surroundings. Each establishment must usually offer at least six bedrooms, and there should be a general bathroom and a general toilet for every six bedrooms without private facilities. Parking facilities should be reasonably close.

Other requirements include a well maintained exterior; clean and hygenic kitchens; a good standard of furnishing; friendly and courteous service; access at reasonable times; the use of a telephone and full breakfast.

A full selection of guesthouses in the area is provided in the AA's annual guide *Guesthouses, Farmhouses and Inns in Britain.*

SELF CATERING

These establishments have to meet minimum standards in accommodation, furniture, fixtures and fittings, services and linen.

Details are to be found in the AA annual guide *Holiday Homes, Cottages, and Apartments in Britain,* which also contains a full selection of self-catering accommodation where indicated in the gazetteer section of this book.

TELEPHONE NUMBERS

Unless otherwise stated, the telephone exchange is that of the town under which the establishment is listed. Where the exchange for a particular establishment is not that of the town under which it appears, the name of the exchange is given before the dialling code and number. In some areas telephone numbers are likely to be changed by the telephone authorities during the currency of this publication. In case of difficulty, check with the operator.

CAUTION

The walks in this book are over private land and do not necessarily follow public rights of way. While landowners usually do not mind visitors using defined routes, care must be taken to ensure that no damage or nuisance is caused to property, animals or wildlife.

It is always advisable to go well-equipped with suitable clothing and refreshments when walking in the Scottish Highlands. The weather can change rapidly, and although most of the walks in this book are not arduous, no walk should be undertaken in adverse conditions.

ORDNANCE SURVEY
LEISURE GUIDE
SCOTTISH HIGHLANDS

**Produced jointly by the Publishing Division of the
Automobile Association and the Ordnance Survey**

Cover: A Highland home in Glen Coe
Back cover: The Grampians, seen from Aviemore
Title page: Ben Lawers and Loch Tay
Opposite: Fishing-net buoys at Buchan
Introductory page: Coire na ciste ski-lifts in the Cairngorms

Editor: Barry Francis

Art Editor: Peter Davies

Editorial contributors: Stewart Angus (Walks), Hamish
Brown (Staying Alive and Walks), Alexander Cameron
(Highland History), Ross Finlay (Gazetteer), Barry
Francis (The Games), Lynn ten Kate (Life on Skye),
Peter MacAuley (Highlands by the Sea), Finlay J
MacDonald (Working in the Top Country), Peter Marren
(Wilderness Wildlife), Dr Robert J Price (Mountain
Landscapes), Alex Sutherland (Walks)

Picture researcher: Wyn Voysey

Original photography: Dennis Hardley,
Ronald W Weir

Printed & bound in Great Britain by
Purnell Book Production Ltd, Paulton, Bristol

Maps extracted from the Ordnance Survey's 1:625,000
Routeplanner enlarged to 1:500,000, 1:25,000 Pathfinder
series, 1:250,000 Routemaster Series, and the
Automobile Association's 1:1,000,000 Map of Great
Britain reduced to 1:1,250,000. Reproduced with the
permission of Her Majesty's Stationery Office. Crown
Copyright Reserved. Additions to the maps by the
Cartographic Unit of the Automobile Association and the
Ordnance Survey.

Produced by the Publishing Division of the Automobile
Association. Distributed in the United Kingdom by the
Ordnance Survey, Southampton, and the Publishing
Division of the Automobile Association, Fanum House,
Basingstoke, Hampshire RG21 2EA.

ISBN 0 86145 236 4 (hardback)   AA Ref 58272
        0 86145 235 6 (softback)   AA Ref 58285
ISBN 0 319 00049 4 (hardback)   OS
        0 319 00050 8 (softback)   OS

Published by the Automobile Association and the
Ordnance Survey.

SCOTTISH HIGHLANDS Introduction

Think of the Scottish Highlands, and you instantly conjure up a vista of heather-clad hills, moody mountains and sparkling lochs, and catch the scented air of open spaces and lofty pines. The guide explores this treasure-house of nature and provides the key to appreciate the many breathtaking attractions in the region. The book traces the history, traditions and geology, lists and describes the towns, villages and hamlets, and offers a wide selection of walks and motor tours to seek out the finest scenery. Written entirely by people who know the region intimately, and backed by the AA's research expertise and the Ordnance Survey's mapping, this guide is as useful to the faithful who return to the Scottish Highlands over and over again as to the first-time visitor.

Highlands History

*S*cottish mountains and glens may be magnificent to view but as places to make a living, they are a harsher environment, different and separate from the Lowlands. Highlands people were considered different, too, as long ago as 1521 when John Major, a Lowlander, called them 'Wild Scots' who spoke the Irish tongue (meaning Gaelic) and kept cattle and sheep. They were always keen for a fight, compared with the Lowlanders who spoke English and were quiet and more civilised, he thought, calling them 'householding Scots'. Yet he praised the Highlanders for their musical tradition using the harp, and particularly for their great love of singing.

People who came by sea

Early people found it much easier to enter the Highlands from the sea. The earliest, of some 5000 to 6000 years ago, have been traced to caves near Oban, where they survived by eating shellfish from the shore and by fishing.

Orkney, only a few miles north of the mainland, was particularly attractive to early settlers – we know that from the abundance of remains to be seen there today. Their houses at Skara Brae were lived in for over 600 years from 3100–2450BC, then covered in sand in a storm and miraculously preserved until they were revealed by another great storm in 1850. The stone houses have a bed on each side of a central hearth; even the furniture, such as the beds and dressers, survives because it was made of stone. Not far away is Maes Howe, the great chambered tomb the settlers built earlier than the Pyramids in Egypt, so big that it is possible to stand up inside and see the chambers in which the family of a great chief was buried. Near it they erected the Ring of Brodgar, a circle

Part of the ornate 7th-century Book of Kells (gospels)

of 60 massive stones, as their place for festivals, on midsummer's day, for example. Similarities in the diameter of this circle and circles at Avebury and the patterns on their pottery connect these farmer-fishers in Orkney with Avebury and Stonehenge in the south of England and they are as early in date.

The Great Glen, which offers a good way across the Highlands by Loch Laggan, Loch Oich and Loch Ness because it never rises much above 100ft, must have been used quite early. At Corriemony, up from Loch Ness, is a chambered cairn inside a circle of 11 standing stones, and at Clava, east of Inverness, are standing stones and chambered cairns, two with entrances aligned on the point where the sun sets on midwinter's day. Kilmartin, not far from the sea in mid-Argyll, also has a remarkable concentration of standing stones and burial cairns. The people who built them understood the calendar, the cardinal points of the compass and had the technology to move large stones close on 5000 years ago: not activities normally conjured up by the term 'wild Scots'.

Stone axes and gold ornaments originating in Ireland but found in the Highlands prove a trading connection lasting all through the bronze age (until about 500BC). Before this, climatic changes to colder and wetter weather restricted the amount of land that could be farmed and saw people fighting for the better land. In the east,

Remains of the enigmatic stone circle at Ben Langas

Blair Castle, built by the powerful Comyn family

people built forts on hills and erected stone walls on a timber framework all round to protect themselves. Several of these were burned, but whether this happened accidentally or was done deliberately, and by whom, are still open questions. Whatever the reason, they burnt at such intense heat that the stones melted and joined together in a solid mass. Two of these vitrified forts worth visiting are Craig Phadrig near Inverness and Tap o' Noth, 1851 ft up near Rhynie in Grampian region.

About 100BC an exciting new kind of stronghold began to appear in the west and north, close to the coast. This was the broch, a round stone tower with double hollow walls, which allowed it to rise to 40ft or more. It has no weak point on the outside, and inside, where there was usually a well, people had a fire to cook on and room to sleep in, safe from the arrow or the hurled spear of the enemy outside. There are no brochs anywhere else in Europe but there are 500 in Scotland. The best examples to visit are Dun Telve and Dun Troddan close together in Glenelg, Dundorilla, close to the north coast, and Struanmore in Skye.

The broch-builders were probably Britons who came by sea from south Britain in the turbulent period before Julius Caesar came. When the Romans entered Scotland they came by land. In the north-east under Agricola they defeated the Caledonians, who must have been mainly Highlanders, in AD 84 at *Mons Graupius,* somewhere close to the Highland Line. The Romans wisely avoided entering the Highland passes and visitors will not see anything Roman in the Highlands. On the other hand, Highlanders occasionally attacked Roman Britain. A Roman writer called them *Picti*, 'the painted men', in AD 297 and all the people in the Highlands came to be known as the Picts until new invaders arrived.

These were the Scots who crossed from Ireland in the 5th and 6th centuries AD and settled in Argyll which became Dalriada, the kingdom of the Scots. They chose *Dunadd,* a fort near Kilmartin, as their capital. On top is a footprint in which a new king on being inaugurated would place his foot as a sign that he would follow faithfully in the path of earlier kings. Gaelic, the language the Scots spoke, gradually spread among all the Highlanders and their name, Scots, in time covered all the people in Scotland.

Christianity also came from Ireland when Columba landed with 12 companions and established a religious centre in Iona. It was they who brought the Gospel to the Highlands. Columba travelled up the Great Glen to Inverness where he met Brude, king of the Picts, and persuaded him to give his protection to the missionaries. Proof of their success in converting the Picts is in the splendid Christian crosses that Pictish sculptors carved on the later symbol-stones in the east and north-east, which are best seen at Aberlemno in Angus. Iona's part in the art of illuminating manuscripts can be judged from the Book of Kells, taken from Iona to Ireland for safety and now in Trinity College, Dublin.

The Vikings from Scandinavia came first as raiders in search of food and treasure, raiding Iona, for example, in 806. Later they settled in Shetland, Orkney and the Western Isles, and on the mainland in Caithness, Wester Ross and Sutherland, which although in the north of Scotland was 'southern land' to the Earls of Orkney. Clues to their settlements occur in place-

names: for example, *setr* meaning a dwelling appears in Tister in Caithness and Uigshader in Skye; and *bolstathr* meaning a farm, in Scrabster in Caithness, Ullapool in Wester Ross, and Skibo and Embo in Sutherland.

Culloden 1746: the beginning of the end of the Highland clans which, with Bonnie Prince Charlie, were crushed by the Duke of Cumberland's troops in their attempt to regain the British Crown. Right: the memorial Cairn

Kings and the Highlands

To survive as king in those times was not easy. Duncan I, a king who was not a Highlander, was killed in battle in 1040 (not murdered in his bed as Shakespeare would have us believe) by Macbeth, the *mormaer* or effective ruler of the north. Macbeth became a strong king until he was defeated and killed by Duncan's son, Malcolm, who became king as Malcolm III.

Attempts by kings to organise Scotland through introducing Norman feudal lords, appointing sheriffs and creating towns had little effect on the Highlands up to about the year 1200. Inverness was unique in being the only burgh, a fortified place with a sheriff to represent the king, and even *his* authority did not extend far. To rule in the West Highlands required a fleet: anyone who had one could behave as if he were a king. Somerled, 'King of the Isles', had one, and used it to sail up the Clyde and challenge the king, Malcolm IV, but he was killed in 1164.

Other families who built advanced stone castles very early in the west were the Stewarts at Rothesay, the MacSweens with Castle Sween in Knapdale, and the Comyns at Inverlochy at the south-west end of the Great Glen. As the Comyns also held Castle Urquhart on Loch Ness at the other end of the Great Glen in 1304, and Ruthven Castle north of the Drumochter Pass (and built the first castle at Blair Atholl to the south of it), they had power right across the Highlands. Robert Bruce had either to befriend them or break them if he wanted to be king. John, 'the Red Comyn', and Bruce quarrelled and Comyn was murdered. Highlanders who fought for Robert I in Scotland's fight for independence, which was won at Bannockburn in 1314, included Mackintoshes, Campbells, MacDonalds and Stewarts.

From Somerled's son, Dougal, came the MacDougalls or sons of Dougal who, based on Dunstaffnage Castle near Oban, were the lords of Lorn; from his son, Ranald, came the family who claimed to be Lords of the Isles until about 1350; and from his grandson, Donald came the great clan of MacDonald, whose leaders were Lords of the Isles until 1492, when James IV was strong enough to bring that position to an end. He could not replace the Lord of the Isles' authority by his own, so this gave the chiefs of clans in the Highlands freedom to behave like little kings.

Chiefs as little kings

The word *clan* means the children and the chief was like an all-powerful father over them. His relatives, who held land directly from him, shared the clan surname and were the clan's chief fighting men, but men with other surnames, like the Macintyres in Clan Campbell, were in the clan because they lived on land the clan had taken. The chief was their judge with the right even to hang them. He was their commander, who could call the clan to war at any time by sending round the 'fiery cross', charred in fire and smeared in blood, and he often did this for feuds with other clans.

In one feud in 1603 Glengarry's men burned a whole congregation of Mackenzies in a church in Easter Ross. Also in 1603 the Macgregors trapped the Colquhouns in Glenfruin and slaughtered 140 of them. This surely was the time of the 'Wild Scots'. James VI outlawed every Macgregor who took part and banned the use of the name. But the Macgregors survived, usually by joining other clans. Rob Roy, who lived on cattle-thieving and protection money a century later, was a Macgregor.

Some Highland clans fought for the Marquis of Montrose in his famous year of victories, 1644–5 during the Civil War, and 50 years later, on the replacement of the Catholic King James VII by the Dutch Protestant William III, it was Highlanders

Proud memorial at Aberfeldy to the Black Watch – the earliest Highland regiment. Many others followed

again who rose and fought under 'Bonnie Dundee' at Killiecrankie in 1689. The treatment of one small clan, the MacDonalds of Glencoe, by Government soldiers who had enjoyed their hospitality for nearly a fortnight in 1692 and then put 38 of them to the sword, lives on in Highland memories as the Massacre of Glencoe.

On the accession of George of Hanover as king of Great Britain in 1714, many Highland chiefs were 'Jacobites', supporters of the exiled Stewarts, and they alone could raise men to fight. A rising in 1715 ended in a drawn battle at Sheriffmuir near Stirling and another was defeated at Glenshiel in 1719. Government troops, Redcoats under General Wade, were then stationed in forts, Fort William, Fort Augustus and Fort George, in the Highlands. They built military roads between the forts and connected them to the Lowlands, and did their best to disarm the Highlanders.

A Highland rising without French help appeared a forlorn hope by 1745 when Prince Charles Edward, grandson of James VII, arrived in the west Highlands with only seven men. Many clans would not rise but MacDonalds and Camerons raised the standards in rebellion at Glenfinnan and swept south, joined by the men of Atholl. They captured Edinburgh and proclaimed the Prince's father king, and penetrated into England as far as Derby, but found no support. After a heroic march, they returned to the Highlands, but at Culloden in 1746 their weary army was no match for the cannon, bayonets and cavalry of the British army under the Duke of Cumberland. Although 'Bonnie Prince Charlie' escaped to France, the days of the 'Wild Scots' were over.

The stamp of government
Redcoats devastated the glens with fire and sword. The Government's new laws prevented Highlanders from possessing weapons of any kind, or wearing kilt, plaid or any garment made of tartan, under pain of transportation. Even the bagpipes were banned as instruments of war.

Jacobite leaders fled and lost their estates.

Every chief lost the right to hold court and try his clansmen. Without it the clan system decayed. No longer a judge, no longer a military leader, the ex-chief was no different from any other landlord.

Highland men could still wear the tartan and fight – but only if they were in the British army! The earliest Highland regiment was the Black Watch, and among the regiments formed by 1800 were the Seaforth Highlanders, the Gordons, the Camerons, the Argylls and the Sutherland Highlanders.

Population and economic change
Traditionally Highlanders depended mainly on keeping cattle for a living, the drovers moving surplus beasts south each year to be sold at Falkirk Tryst. Good land was scarce and as population increased, the potato was a new crop which kept many of them alive, but famine struck sometimes, as it did so distressingly in 1846.

Farmers from the south would pay rents that were three times higher for the land as big sheep-farms, once the glens had been cleared. This happened on a large scale in Sutherland. In Strathnaver in 1819, for example, people had to move, as their houses were burned to make sure they did not return. Given small plots on a wild coast, they were told to make a living by fishing.

The number of Highlanders emigrating rose alarmingly by 1800 and the engineer, Thomas Telford, suggested a great public works programme – building roads, bridges, harbours and the Caledonian Canal – to create jobs and open up the Highlands. The work went on under him for twenty years, and the Canal, the roads and many of the thousand bridges are still in use today. Tourists came in but industry did not, even after the construction of railways later in the century.

After the sheep came the creation of sporting estates, especially deer forests in Inverness-shire, Skye and Wester Ross, as a cause of clearance and depopulation. The ruins of deserted settlements can be seen in empty glens but where did all the people go? Some were moved to meagre crofts on the coast, some went to industrial towns in the south, great numbers emigrated to make a new life in Canada and the United States, and later to Australia and New Zealand.

Since 1945, hydro-electricity has made houses more comfortable in the Highlands, and light industries possible. These, together with forestry and tourism have provided new jobs, whereas larger industries have been less successful. The Highlands and Islands Development Board supports ventures which will bring work to the Highlands, a place where people are conscious of their past, but where there is room to grow.

Kilmorack power station, transforming Highland life

Mountain Landscapes

*T*he Scottish Highlands contain some of the grandest scenery in Europe, and, taken together, the landscapes of northern Scotland form one of the largest-surviving 'wilderness' areas in the Western hemisphere.

Look at a map of the British islands and a cursory glance will show that the north of Scotland is as big in area as East Anglia, the Midlands and the Home Counties put together. And yet the population is small in number, and most of it is concentrated within the towns.

That such a huge area remains almost empty and largely 'wild' (from long, deep sea-lochs penetrating far inland in the south-west, to dramatic volcanic rock cliffs on the Inner Hebrides) is remarkable when you think that northern Europe is one of the most crowded and 'developed' parts of the world. And it is the erosion, by rivers and glaciers, of the ancient rocks underlying this vast area that explains much of its appearance and character.

How the Highlands evolved

When seeing the mountains ahead, visitors approaching the Highlands from the south or south-east know immediately why the area is given this name. The boundary between the Highlands and the Lowlands of Scotland is quite definite. It runs roughly twenty miles north of Glasgow, Stirling, Perth and Montrose, continues north then west, leaving out much of Aberdeenshire and the lower lands along the Moray Firth to Inverness.

To understand the evolution of the Highland scenery we have to think in terms of four time scales. Firstly, the most ancient rocks developed between 300 million and 3000 million years ago. These metamorphic rocks, as they are known, are tough materials which have been compressed, baked and twisted, and lie beneath large areas of the Highlands. During this long phase of early geological history there were several periods of mountain building. In some ways the present mountain scenery can be regarded as the worn-down roots of a much larger, ancient mountain system. Secondly, during the last 100 million years, two very significant events occurred – a period of volcanic activity and the development of a river valley network. Thirdly, during the last two million years, there have been frequent and dramatic changes in the climate, resulting in what is generally known as the 'ice-age'. On at least 20 occasions the climate deteriorated so much that glaciers developed in the Highlands. Fourthly, the last 30,000 years have produced obvious changes in Highland landscapes, due largely to the build up and eventual disappearance of the last ice sheet to cover Scotland. Each of these phases has left its mark on the character of Highland scenery.

Rocks and structures

In the north-west mainland and in the Outer Hebrides, large areas are made up of gneiss. This rock, which probably lies under the younger rocks of much of the rest of the Highlands, was formed

Cloud-tipped Ben Slioch from the shore of Loch Maree

over 2000 million years ago and often shows a distinctive banding, visible in various forms. In northern Lewis it underlies gently undulating areas, while in southern Lewis and western Sutherland it forms mountains.

A younger formation of metamorphic rocks occupies the south-east Highlands from Kintyre to Buchan. Called the Dalradian system, it is the main constituent of the Grampians and tends to produce smooth slopes and rounded summits. About 400 million years ago great upheavals occurred in what is known, in almost Hollywood-sounding terms, as the 'Caledonian Mountain Building Episode'. At that time great mountain chains, at least the size of the present European Alps and possibly similar in size to the Himalayas, were created by the earth's crust folding and splitting.

It was at this time that the basic 'grain' of the Highlands was established, and the Great Glen and Highland Boundary faults developed.

As the illustration shows, there are numerous outcrops of granite throughout the Highlands and Islands. Granite is most common in the Grampians, but significant outcrops also occur in Arran, Mull, Skye, Harris, Lewis and Sutherland. In most cases the granite forms rugged mountains, as in Arran and Skye, but in the Cairngorms the granite underlies smooth, flat surfaces. Most of the granites were thrust up about 500 million years ago, except for those of Skye, Mull and Arran, which were associated with volcanic activity some 60 million years ago.

Sedimentary rocks occupy only a relatively small part of the area of the Highlands and Islands. Apart from small outcrops in places such as Mull, Morven and Arran, there are two main areas: a coastal zone 10 to 20 miles wide stretching from Cape Wrath to the Sound of Sleat, and an east-coast area extending from around the shores of the Moray Firth through Caithness to Orkney. These two have very different geological characters. The western area consists of palaeozoic sandstone and limestone, which are 500 to 800 million years old, whereas the eastern area consists of Devonian sandstone and shales 350 to 400 million years old.

Contrasts

There are remarkable differences in the north-west Highlands, between the two base rocks – the Lewisian gneiss and the overlying sandstone. The Torridonian sandstone is the oldest sedimentary rock within the region and is known to be over 1600ft thick.

The best examples of these sediments are the pyramid-like mountains of Ross and Sutherland – Suilven, Quinag, and the massive, stepped mountains of the Torridon district.

The main sediments occur only to the west of one of the most distinctive structures in Scotland – the Moine Thrust. This consists of a series of faults along which great masses of rock have been moved many miles north-westwards. A major feature resulting from these thrusts are westward-facing escarpments that have been produced as a result of erosion of the rocks.

While the western area of sedimentary rocks has great mountain and valley systems, the eastern area – occupied by Devonian sediments – is characterised either by lowlands (around the shores of the Moray Firth, Caithness and most of the Orkney Islands), or by smooth, rounded hills. It is quite likely that at one time these sediments extended much further to the west, particularly in Sutherland, but were gradually removed by erosion.

The last dramatic geological event, resulting in the accumulation of solid rock in the Highlands and Islands, occurred about 60 million years ago. Major centres of volcanic activity occurred in Skye, Rhum, Ardnamurchan, Mull and Arran, creating extensive flows of basalt lava. Thick accumulations of this form much of north-west Mull, Morven, and the fantastic towers and pinnacles of the Storr of Skye and the sinister fangs of the Black Cuillins. Wherever these lavas occur they form a distinctive 'stepped' landscape.

It seems likely that the Highlands were up-lifted some 50 million years ago, in the form of a gently-sloping eroded surface with a general tilt to the south-east. In what is believed to have been a sub-tropical climate, a drainage system developed with the longest rivers flowing towards the east and south-east.

The basic framework of Highland scenery was established during the Tertiary Period (up to 70 million years ago), but because of the intensity of erosion during the Pleistocene Period, little is known about the details of the land's evolution during this critical period.

Metamorphic rocks

- Dalradian schist
- Moinian schist
- Lewisian gneiss

Igneous rocks

- Extrusive lava
- Intrusive lava

Sedimentary rocks

- Mesozoic sediments – sandstones, shales, limestones
- Old red sandstone
- Cambrian sediments
- Torridonian sandstone

---------- Major faults

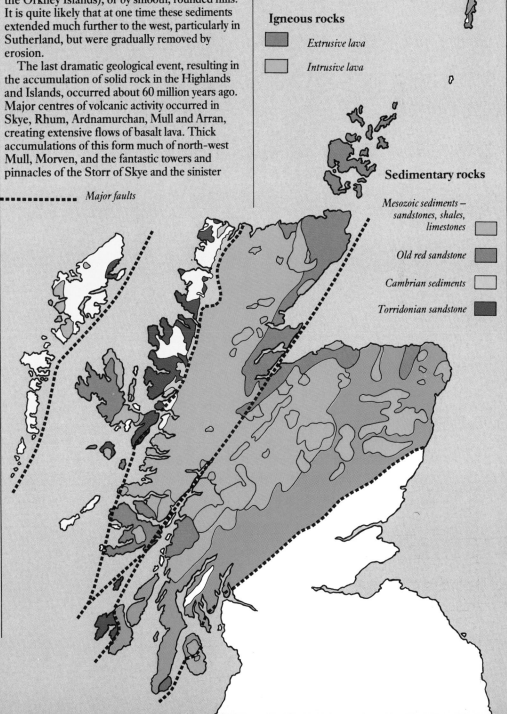

The effects of glaciation

During the last two million years the world's climate has undergone frequent and dramatic changes, which in northern latitudes have allowed glaciers and ice sheets to develop; hence the 'ice-age'. There were, in fact, numerous (maybe 20) periods, each lasting about 100,000 years when mean temperatures in Scotland during January fell by 5° to 10° C – conditions in which it would have been possible for glaciers to develop.

Events in geological history can be interpreted only from the deposits and forms these events left behind. Because glaciation produces only loosely-packed sediments, it is not surprising that, except in certain favoured localities, the deposits of earlier glaciations were destroyed by later glaciers. How many times the Scottish ice sheet built up and then retreated is not known (possibly as many as 20 times). Most of what we know about the glaciation of Scotland is based on the evidence relating to the last ice sheet which began to develop about 27,000 years ago and which finally wasted away about 10,000 years ago.

What is a glacier?

A period of glaciation starts when the snow line (the level at which the snow remains from one winter to the next), is progressively lowered. Within the Highlands and Islands, the main area of ice accumulation coincided with the zone of high ground stretching from Cape Wrath to the Firth of Clyde. These west-facing slopes had heavy falls of snow, until permanent snow banks began to form on the high ground and in the valley heads. As the climate became worse, the snow banks thickened and the snow was converted to glacier ice. In the early stages, glaciers were confined by valleys, but eventually they became so thick that even the intervening ridges were buried and an ice-cap built up. While the main ice-cap was developing in the western mountains of the mainland, other local centres of ice accumulation developed on the islands of Harris, Skye, Rhum, Mull and Arran in the west, and in the Cairngorms and Monadliath Mountains in the east. The ice

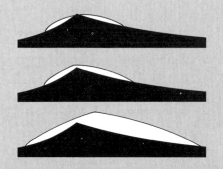

As snow banks thickened they turned to glacier ice. This eventually became so thick that intervening ridges were buried and ice caps built up

Burnside view of Ben Bhàn on the road to Applecross

moved outwards from these centres, the lines of movement being recorded by fragments of rock which can be found in the glacial deposits known as 'erratics' (pieces of rock which do not occur locally but have been transported from another area by a glacier).

The various centres of ice accumulation eventually joined to produce an ice-sheet which completely buried all the Highlands and Islands. It is unlikely that even the highest peaks stood above the surface of the ice, because the highest parts of the ice probably reached altitudes of about 5000ft. Individual ice-streams within the ice-sheet were up to 3000ft thick and probably moved at rates of between 30 and 600ft per year. This

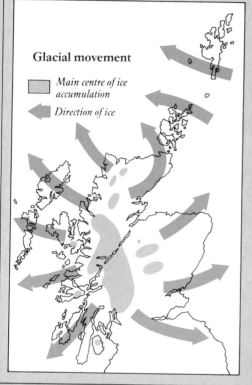

Glacial movement

Main centre of ice accumulation

Direction of ice

ice-sheet reached its maximum extent about 18,000 years ago and by 13,000 years ago had disappeared. Then, about 11,000 years ago, a sharp deterioration of climate allowed the build up of glaciers in the western Highlands and in other areas of high ground.

Glacier ice itself is not very hard but, as nearly all glaciers pick up fragments of rock in their lower layers, the underside is rather like a piece of sandpaper. As the glaciers move forward under the force of gravity, they erode and scoop out the rock surfaces of the valley heads over which they pass, to produce 'armchair' hollows known as cirques or corries. As ice moves, the sides of the valleys tend to be straightened and steepened, and the floors deepened. A typical glaciated valley is trough-like with straight, steep sides and with a basin gouged out of its floor. Some of these ice-gouged basins are very deep: Loch Morar 1017ft, Loch Ness 754ft and Loch Lomond 623ft, for example.

As they grind along, glaciers carry the eroded material over and within the ice and re-deposit it. When the ice melts, the transported material is released to form a characteristically unsorted debris and boulder clay called till. These deposits are to be found extensively in the Highlands and Islands and are an important surface material on the lower slopes of even the highest areas. The amount of debris is sometimes so great that the glacier ice becomes completely buried with boulders, gravel, sand and clay. Eventually the ice beneath the material melts and a series of hills 10 to 50ft high is produced. These morainic mounds give a wild appearance to the floor of many a Highland glen.

Outlook: warmer and wetter

When the glaciers of the Highlands began to melt, vast quantities of water were released. The lower ends of some valleys remained blocked by ice while the upper ends were ice free. This allowed large, deep lakes to develop with glacier ice acting

The Pass of the Cattle looking toward Loch Kishorn

There may be snow on distant peaks, but Kilchurn Castle and Loch Awe lie warm in the autumn sunshine

as a dam. The most famous example within the Highlands was in Glen Roy (north of Fort William), where the lake lasted sufficiently long for shorelines to develop along the valley side.

The obvious routes for most of the meltwaters to follow during the retreat of the glaciers were the valley floors. The rivers we now see in the Highland glens increased in volume many times during the summer melt periods. These swollen rivers deposited large quantities of boulders, gravel and sand on the valley floor, and subsequently the rivers began to cut into these deposits to produce the fine river terraces seen in many Highland glens.

As the glaciers began to retreat from the Highlands during the last glaciation, the land was still so depressed by the weight of the ice that the sea level, astonishingly, was relatively higher than it is today. Around many parts of the Highland coastline, evidence of this phenomenon can be seen by the remains of marine platforms, cliff lines and raised beaches.

The age of ice came to an end some 10,000 years ago, and with the improving climate, the Highlands were rapidly colonised by oak, birch and pine. The landscape encountered by the earliest humans (about 8000 years ago) was very different from that of today. In the following centuries man was to transform the Highlands from forest to moorland, but that is another story . . .

Wilderness Wildlife

So far as we know, all the wild plant and animal life in the Highlands have colonised the area during the past 15,000 years. The bare debris of gravel left behind after the ice age was first clothed with vegetation characteristic of the Scandinavian tundra – mosses, scrubby willows and dwarf birches and hardy plants, such as heather and crowberry. In time, a taller forest of birch and juniper developed, and the trees of more temperate climates, such as Scots pine, oak, hazel, alder and ash, gradually spread in from the lowlands as the land mellowed under the warm post-glacial sun. When man first appeared as a hunter-gatherer in the Highlands, about 8000 years ago, all except the highest and wettest land may have been covered by trees. The 'Caledonian Forest' of Scots pine covered much of the drier soils of the eastern Highlands. In the milder, more humid climate of the west, oak dominated the lower slopes but in the harsher peatland landscape of the far north, woodland may have been confined to nooks of deep soil in the coastal glens. Sutherland and Caithness probably never supported much more than an open scrub of birch, juniper and willow.

Disappearing wildlife

We have lost much of the wildlife of those ancient forests. Lynx, bear, elk and wild cattle disappeared long ago, but wild reindeer survived in the far north until the 12th century and beaver until the 16th, while the last Highland wolf perished as recently as 1743. The forests themselves were long protected by their remoteness. But the 'taming' of the Highlands during the 18th century began a period of over-exploitation with profound results to the scenery and wildlife. The smelting industry of the west coast converted many of the finest oaks to charcoal while the tallest pines of the east were felled and sent down river to the timber markets. There was little respite for young trees to replace their sires, for animals were put into the woods to graze while flockmasters deliberately burned woods to extend their sheep ranges. Stocking the hills with red deer for the Victorian sportsman further limited the regeneration of the natural woods, and were it not for plantings by enlightened owners to replace them, the hills would be bare indeed. The loss of the Caledon Forest caused widespread soil erosion and improverishment, particularly in the west, and the resultant bare, boney landscape of today has often been called a 'wet desert' in consequence. It presents a spectacle of stark beauty to the visitor, but it is a haunted landscape for it once contained both trees and men.

Woodland – old and new

Today's Highlands contain more woodland than at any time since the 18th century, but most of this consists of young plantations of imported conifers, monotonous to look at and even more monotonous to walk through. Naturalists seek out the fragments of older, more natural woods which are,

fortunately, still quite extensive in certain parts of the Highlands. The most famous of these are the old pine-woods, whose sonorous names – Rannoch, Rothiemurchus, Ballochbuie, Abernethy and Glen Affric – conjure up images of primaeval mossy groves, carpeted with blaeberry, in which crested tits forage among the juniper and capercaillies swell and strut like ancestral turkeycocks. There *are* such places in the Highlands but they have to be sought; the visitor must abandon his car and be prepared to walk several miles, but the rewards can be great. Eagles still nest on trees in some of the eastern pinewoods and buzzards are quite frequent. The Scottish crossbill, a colourful, parrot-like finch whose curiously shaped bill is

A chequered skipper at rest. Normally its quick, darting flight makes it a difficult butterfly to observe

designed to extract seed from pine cones, is found nowhere else in the world. In the boggy clearings in some of the Speyside pinewoods, greenshank nest among the heather. And, the lucky visitor will catch a glimpse of a wildcat or even a pine marten, for these beautiful mammals have increased their range since the days when the gin-trap brought them to the brink of extinction in Scotland.

The Highlands contain types of other 'wild wood' which probably resemble the original forest quite closely. Rassal Ashwood, in Ross, is a tangle of cankered old trees, twisting over mossy blocks of limestone. In the spring, it rings to the song of warbler, tit, robin and thrush, a green oasis of bustle in the wind-swept moor. Morrone Birkwood, near Braemar, is one of our few surviving Alpine woods, where mountain flowers, spangling the grass beneath the miniature birch trees, recall the remote Highland spring which followed the age of ice. The oakwoods of the west coast, on the shores of Loch Sunart and the Sound of Jura, are lush and humid compared with woods further east. Their floors are carpeted with ferns and herb-rich grassland in which the abundant butterflies include the beautiful pearl-bordered fritillary and the rare chequered skipper. But the features which place these woods in international renown are their mosses and lichens which plaster the bark and festoon the branches with their feathery or seaweed-like growths.

Going up

But as a visitor to the Highlands you will seek not the woods but the hills. On the way to the high tops, you will pass through several zones of moorland vegetation – heather, mat-grass, deer-grass, each punctuated by boggy runnels and depressions spotted with the white flowers of cloudberry, the mountain bramble, and the red and green cushions of Sphagnum moss. You will hear the sounds of the hill – the sibilant call of the meadow pipit, the melancholy pipe of the golden

plover and, above all, the bubbling cry of the curlew. In the east, these moorland areas are dominated by heather, which forms a glorious flowering mantle of royal purple in August, before assuming its mellow autumn colours. In the spring, many heather moors will be striped with small burned patches. Burning is the traditional way of maintaining the moor, for heather can grow faster than animals can graze it and, if left unmanaged, it becomes dry and 'leggy'. Fire produces a young, more nutritious sward, which can support higher densities of red grouse and grazing animals.

The red grouse is the most familiar bird of the heather moors and plays an important part in the economy of Highland estates. The size of the burned patch is designed to coincide with the territory of a cock bird and a well-maintained moor will contain many more nesting pairs than one which has been allowed to become run down and neglected. Grouse moors are also the best places to see mountain hares, which are more thick-set than their lowland relative, with bigger heads and shorter ears. In the summer, the

Golden eagle and chick in their remote mountain eyrie

One of the lush and humid oak woodlands in Argyll

mountain hare has a coat of brownish-grey fur, but it moults in the autumn to produce its snow-white raiment. A hare looks absurdly conspicuous on the brown hillside in years when the snow melts early, however.

On the wing
Flying insects are always a feature of the Scottish moors although those which press their attentions most persistently are the clegs and midges which plague the boggy districts of the north and west. Altogether more attractive are the two mountain butterflies, the mountain ringlet and the large heath which fly – or are blown – over bare hillsides, sometimes accompanied by large day-flying moths such as the emperor, Scotland's only wild silk-moth, and the northern eggar. Many Highland moths have a life-cycle of two years or more, perhaps an insurance against the fickle Highland summer. One particularly beautiful moth, the Kentish glory (which, despite its name, is confined to the Highlands) can remain in its cocoon for up to seven years.

Most visitors to the Scottish moors will see red deer. The best season is autumn when the stags become fiercely territorial and the browning hills

Pearl-bordered fritillary: a mainly woodland butterfly with a rapid flight

echo to their eerie roars. Deer come to lower ground in the winter to shelter in their ancestral habitat, the wooded glens. Hungry deer will raid gardens and crop fields in winter and west coast animals will even eat seaweed. The hinds wander less far than stags, and retire in the spring to calve in remote corries. The Highland red deer are free-ranging wild animals, although most of them are descended from introduced European stock. On lower ground, some estates now farm deer for venison within large fenced paddocks. But the wild deer will be a valuable asset to the Highland estate so long as there are people who are prepared to pay to stalk them.

Mountain flowers
Eventually we reach the heady air of the high tops. Beautiful, and perhaps unfamiliar, flowers will soon catch the eye. The mountain environment poses many problems for wild flowers. They must endure cold and high winds, scant or infertile soil, a short growing season, heavy rain and, conversely, severe drought: in a typical Highland summer, a plant may be frosted one day and exposed to drying winds the next. Consequently some flowers grow in tight rosettes or mats, and this growth habit, which combines small leathery leaves with large, colourful flowers, gives us some of our most attractive species. In the Cairngorms, the pink stars of moss campion and trailing azalea are among the few bright colours in the stony desert of the plateau. Other plants seek sheltered pockets of deep soil in the gullies and ledges of

Fearsomely aggressive, night-hunting wildcats are not all bad – they keep down the number of small animals that damage trees

steep cliffs. Such places have much in common with the dark, moist floor of rocky woodlands, and, indeed, woodland flowers like red campion and wood sorrel are commonly found high up on the mountains. Curiously enough, the now ubiquitous rosebay willow-herb originated as a plant of mountain cliffs and was once regarded as a rarity. Frost-sensitive mountain ferns grow in places covered by snow until late in the season, for beneath the snow the plants are protected from wind and extreme cold.

Some mountains possess a much richer flora than others. Hills like Ben Lawers in Perthshire and Caenlochan in Angus are justifiably famous as 'botanical Meccas' although there are many other less-famous hills which are almost as rewarding. Ben Lawers is composed of lime-rich rocks which weather to form deep, fertile soils, and support grass rather than heather. It therefore appears from a distance as a green hill, contrasting strongly with nearby Schiehallion and the hills of Rannoch whose granites and quartzites form poorer soils and whose flanks are clad with heather. The hanging rock gardens of Ben Lawers are resplendent with the jewel-like flowers of mountain saxifrages, gentians, forget-me-nots,

speedwells and mouse-ears. In the past, some of their admirers sought these plants with trowels and sacks. Mountain flowers include some of our rarest species and should be left in their magnificent setting for everyone to enjoy.

High flyers
Only a small number of birds are hardy enough to nest on the high tops and, of these, the ptarmigan

Branches everywhere: the magnificent red deer stag (here about 7 years old) is Britain's largest wild animal, standing 4 ft high at the shoulder

is the most conspicuous. There are said to be only two roads in the Highlands which pass through ptarmigan territory. In the spring, the displaying cock birds soar upwards and descend on rapidly beating wings, giving vent to belch-like croaks. They are unusually 'tame' birds, confident in their hostile domain, and will usually allow the visitor to approach within a few yards; they even seem at home on crowded ski-slopes. Much rarer than the ptarmigan is the dotterel, a beautiful arctic plover which visits the high tops in summer. The dotterel's nesting behaviour is unusual in that it is the cock which incubates the eggs while the hen defends the territory. In the Cairngorms you may also hear the sweet song of the snow bunting. Every summer, a few of these attractive finches remain to nest among the boulder fields of the

high plateau, which so resembles their main breeding grounds in the arctic tundra. But more often they are seen in flocks, aptly known as 'snowflakes', in the early spring, feeding on ski-resort crumbs like suburban sparrows before their long journey north.

Rose bay willow-herb entwined with bindweed

Highland fish

The waters of Highland rivers and lochs are cold and clear. Salmon 'run' up fast-flowing rivers like the Dee and Spey to their spawning grounds in the gravel reaches in the heart of the Highlands. Trout, on the other hand, are common in most lochs and streams. Some of the deep mountain lochs also contain char, a beautiful red and black relative of the trout, whose isolated breeding pools have nurtured a large number of different races. Accompanying the char in some of these cold, remote places is the 'ferox' trout, a heavy variety with large black spots against a background of deep gold. The dark, mysterious freshwaters of the Highlands have attracted their share of legend; the monster, which may or may not inhabit Loch Ness, has his counterpart in the 'kelpies' who dwell in the allegedly bottomless 'pots' of deep rivers. They take the form of aquatic horses, oxen or beings of more devilish appearance, with horns and eyes like hot coals.

Every Highland river eventually reaches the sea, and the west coast, with its gaunt, craggy headlands, its sweet, secluded sea lochs thronged with marine life, and its sand and shingle strands is a paradise for the naturalist. On the north coast, blown sand may support buttercups, clover, eyebrights, stork's-bills and wild pansies in a springy herbal carpet known as machair. At Durness in Sutherland, plants normally found on mountains, such as mountain avens and bearberry, spill over on to the dunes in a spectacle of wild colour. These are among the last places on the mainland where one can regularly hear (but seldom see) corncrakes among the scented fields.

Salmon can leap falls 11ft high, taking off at 20mph

Island colonies

The most spectacular bird colonies are to be found on the off-shore islands. Handa, near the Sutherland coast, has steep cliffs with horizontal ledges crowded with thousands of guillemots, razorbills, kittiwakes and fulmars. The mountainous island of Rhum, often said to look from a distance like a basket of eggs, possesses a huge colony of Manx shearwaters which nest in burrows in the soft soils of the mountainsides. Shearwaters are ocean birds which come to land only at night. It is an unforgettable experience to hear the raucous screams of the unseen birds as they circle about your head and land with a soft 'flump' before scurrying off into the darkness.

Islay is another rewarding island. The steep cliffs of the Mull of Oa are the Scottish home of the chough (pronounced 'chuff') perhaps the most attractive and certainly the rarest of the crow family, and also one of the world's strongholds for the rare Greenland races of white-fronted and barnacle goose.

The future

What of the future of Highland wildlife? Some indications are encouraging, others less so. Many of the finest remaining wild places are protected as nature reserves by the Nature Conservancy Council, the Royal Society for the Protection of Birds and the Scottish Wildlife Trust. Some of the most spectacular animals, such as grey seal, red squirrel and wild cat are more widespread and numerous today than they were at the turn of the century. The osprey has returned to Scotland and so too, with a little help from the Nature Conservancy, has the magnificent white-tailed

Fulmars soar effortlessly on long, narrow wings

eagle. Moral attitudes have changed for the better: few of us nowadays would care to shoot a rare falcon or fill a hamper with rare mountain ferns. Depite some unfortunate local developments, modern tourism has not seriously harmed Highland wildlife, and there is every reason, given sensible planning policies, to suppose that the two are compatible.

On the debit side, an increasing proportion of the Highlands is passing out of the hands of the traditional families and clans and into those of institutions and financiers whose motives are primarily one of profit. One such effect has been the afforestation of peat bogs, hardly suitable for trees but of great importance for breeding birds, in the flow country of Sutherland and Caithness. Ugly, bulldozed tracks, designed mainly to save industrialist stalkers the use of their legs, have scarred many a Highland fastness, while the native woodlands are steadily dwindling in extent through poor management and the over-grazing of deer, cattle and sheep. A still more insidious menace is acid rain, a looming threat to soils, to trees, to fish and, above all, to the unique lichen flora of the western woods.

Problems such as those have no simple solution. But in many ways, the visitor who wishes to see Highland wildlife has never had it so good. Information centres will have details of the many long-distance footpaths, nature trails and areas of special interest which are available for the traveller. The basic rules are: leave your car behind, take sensible precautions against bad weather and rough ground, and treat what you find with respect. The Scottish Highlands is one of the last wildernesses of Europe; it has enriched the spirit of many an earlier traveller; let it do the same for you.

Highlands by the Sea

*S*uch is the splendour of its moorland and mountain, loch and glen that, in terms of natural beauty, Scotland is comparable with any part of the world. So familiar are these attractions, however, that there is one important feature that is overlooked –the country's Highland seaside. Many people head from Britain's south coast or make the long haul abroad every year to be beside the seaside, but how many of them are aware of the number of attractive beaches in the north of Scotland?

Skye's the limit

The rugged coastline to the west separates the mainland from the serene Isle of Skye, where the magnificent Cuillin Hills and majestic mountains contrast strongly with the sandy beaches nestling beneath them.

The beaches at Glen Brittle and Camasunary are in an area from which mountain rescue

The small Buchan fishing village of Pennan, on a rocky coastal stretch overlooked by Pennan Head

operations are often co-ordinated. Camasunary is best reached via Elgol, following a rough track, best suited to Land Rovers or similar four-wheel-drive vehicles. Across the waters of Loch Scavaig and Loch Slapin lies the safe and sandy beach at Tarskavaig, in the picturesque parish of Sleat. The main centre of Skye is Portree, which is about 34 miles from the ferry terminal at Kyle of Lochalsh. This a pleasant, bustling village, which has a wide range of shops and hotels, as well as bed and breakfast accommodation.

Across the blustery Minch, in lovely Wester Ross, the Gairloch peninsula boasts several beaches, all within a relatively short distance of one another. For many people Wester Ross holds particular charm. The traditional way of life seems to remain unaffected by time, in contrast with other areas which have played host to high-wage industries such as oil-platform construction yards. There is such a yard on the shores of Loch Kishorn, giving much needed employment to both locals and 'outsiders'.

Passing by Badachro, on Loch Gairloch, leads to Red Point beach. This is a delightful area, sheltered from the hustle and bustle of other areas because the road reaches a dead end here. The Badachro peninsula is very popular with holidaymakers because it offers even more seclusion than other villages. There is easy access to Gairloch, which offers plenty of opportunity and facilities for sailing. Every summer, there is a regatta which attracts many entries from locals and visitors.

Museum of the year

There is a museum at Gairloch giving a fascinating insight into the area's way of life throughout the ages. It is run by the Gairloch Heritage Society and is proving to be so successful that the society is now looking for bigger premises. In recent years, it won a joint award as Scotland's museum of the year.

On the road to Melvaig (another dead end) there is an impressive beach at Big Sand, with caravan facilities nearby. There are no problems with parking here, or indeed anywhere else in the north of Scotland. There are a lot of wide open spaces – and not a parking meter in sight.

There is a generous selection of hotels and bed and breakfast accommodation on offer in the Gairloch area, too. The village itself has several hotels, of different size, as well as traditional bars which retain a taste of yesteryear. And, just for good measure, there is a fine, sandy beach at Gairloch itself with a magnificent view over towards the north end of the Isle of Skye.

Travelling from Gairloch towards Aultbea, there is a chance to pass through Poolewe, and enjoy a walk through the Inverewe Gardens. Every year thousands of people visit these sub-tropical gardens, which are run by the National Trust for Scotland.

Near Aultbea, there is a magnificent beach at Mellon Udrigle, secluded and sheltered on the shore of Gruinard Bay. This, again, is a tiny village, with its inhabitants making a living off the land. Towards Inverasdale, there is a beach at Firemore, where visitors can park – even with caravans – without problems.

By the main road towards Dundonnell, there is a superb stretch of sand at the head of Gruinard Bay, which attracts many people each summer. This is the typical picture postcard setting which

The north-west coastline of Skye – the Misty Isle

people are immediately attracted to. The fact that Gruinard island, about a mile offshore, was contaminated by anthrax spores during experiments by Ministry of Defence in 1942 does not, apparently, keep people away! There are notices by the shore warning the public that they are not allowed to visit the island.

The quiet life

Further north in Ross and Cromarty, toward Achiltibuie, there are more beaches in the Coigeach area. Achiltibuie is a quiet, even isolated, spot, offering tranquillity to those who are keen to desert the city life for a while. Achiltibuie itself offers a fine beach, and there is another further north toward the tip of the Coigeach peninsula, at Achnahaird. This is another beach with a lot to offer, and parking is no problem. Although this is a scattered community, Achiltibuie has hotels and shops which cater for most people's holiday needs.

Over the border

Crossing the border into the county of Sutherland, several pleasant beaches can be found. Near the village of Scourie, there is a stretch of sand towards Tarbet. Just off the coast, there is a bird sanctuary on Handa Island, popular with ornithologists. Scourie, again, has the facilities one can expect in a small Highland community.

Amid the magnificent scenery of Oldshoremore to the north lie some delightful beaches which are well worth a visit. They are close to the bustling fishing village of Kinlochbervie, which is earmarked as being one of the main fishing centres in the Highlands in the years to come.

Towards Cape Wrath, on the far north-west corner of Scotland, the visitor should take in the historic settlement of Durness, which has beaches nearby. The countryside here is isolated but incredibly beautiful and remains totally unspoilt by modern development. Indeed, it is so unspoilt that some locals want the absentee owners of the various estates to put in some effort, not to mention money, into a programme of regeneration to revitalise the community.

Along the north coastal road, taking in the Kyle of Tongue, are scenes of idyllic splendour. There are yet more beaches by the Kyle of Tongue, where wildlife abounds.

Coming into Caithness from Sutherland, the

traveller comes to the sands at Reay, on the edge of Sandside Bay. This is quite close to the atomic reactor at Dounreay, about eight miles from the town of Thurso. This is a fairly big town by Highland standards, and has a rail link with Inverness, the capital of the Highlands. To the east of Thurso are the Dunnett Sands, at Dunnett Bay. Near Thurso lies the port and fishing harbour of Scrabster, from which there is a ferry service to the Orkney Islands.

Just a few miles from Thurso there is Castle of Mey, the Queen Mother's holiday home. Down the east coast of Caithness, on the shore of Sinclair's Bay, are the extensive Reiss sands.

Back on to the east coast of Sutherland are all the principal towns such as Golspie, Brora and Dornoch, and they offer pleasant beaches. Dornoch in particular, as befits the main town in the county of Sutherland, has very prominent beaches, alongside a championship golf course. The town has a number of good hotels, with fine views out over the North Sea and to the Dornoch Firth. The quaint little village of Embo nearby also has a beach, as well as a caravan site, alongside Granny's Heilan Hame, a well-known place for *ceilidhs* – Gaelic for a get-together.

Return to Ross

Back into Ross and Cromarty – and there is no shortage of beaches in Easter Ross: Tain, Portmahomack, Hilton, Inver, Balintore and Shandwick, and they are all quite close to one another. Tain, the biggest of these, is an ancient royal burgh with full shopping and accommodation facilities, as well as a golf course. Easter Ross is primarily a farming community and nowadays the only large-scale heavy industry is the oil-platform construction yard at Nigg Bay, on the shores of Cromarty Firth. It is flat and very fertile land, in total contrast to Wester Ross with its rugged scenery.

The Black Isle area of Ross and Cromarty is

Fishing nets drying at Cruden Bay – a resort noted for its fine sand and championship golf course

fertile farming land, too. This is not an island at all, but a peninsula, with new bridges both north and south built within the last six years, making it an excellent centre with easy access to the main roads. It has beaches at Rosemarkie and Fortrose, with a golf course and a caravan site nearby. This is a very popular and relaxing area for the tourist, with Inverness only 15 minutes drive away.

On the other side of the Moray Firth, there is a very good beach for caravanners at Nairn, which is a bustling town offering good hotels and accommodation.

Further along to the east, there is a prominent beach at Findhorn, close to the RAF station at Kinloss. This goes along to Roseisle and then there is a long beach at Lossiemouth, which is again in the shadow of an RAF station. In Banff and Buchan district, there is a beach at Sandend (between Portsoy and Cullen); with a small beach and caves at Cullykhan, between Gardenstown and Pennan. There are also beaches at Fraserburgh and Peterhead, both towns which grew out of the fishing industry.

Capital beaches

Coming into Aberdeen, Scotland's oil capital, there is a beautiful sandy beach stretching from Aberdeen, through to Balmedie and on to Newburgh – about 10 miles of sandy beach in all. Coloured markers are provided for safety. At Balmedie, there is a good opportunity for bird watchers to indulge in their hobby.

At the southern end of the beach, toward the city, there are cafés, discos and amusement arcades, in what is said to be the largest permanent such arcade in Scotland. For those seeking the quiet life, however, the rest of the beach is unspoilt. As one person from the tourist office said: 'There is amusement there for those who want it. For those who don't want that, there are miles of unspoilt beaches.' As for Aberdeen itself . . . well, it may certainly have grown and made a name for itself in the oil world, but many people who know the city well maintain that it has retained its character in spite of all that.

The Games

steep hillsides) could be carried out with the minimum of equipment, but as a change from slaving over a hot anvil, blacksmiths would see how far they could throw their hammers or iron weights. Well-rounded stones, suitable for 'putting' were retrieved from fast-flowing rivers. Forest workers used a branch-stripped tree trunk (*caber* in Gaelic) for their own trial of strength and skill.

'Ye casting of ye bar', as tossing the caber was once known, is perhaps the most remarkable and thrilling of all the events. The straight, heavy pine trunk (the Braemar caber is almost 20ft long and weighs 132 lb) is grasped vertically in the competitor's cupped hands at its smaller end. The object is to heave the tapering caber with a mighty jerk on to its thicker end so that it describes a semi-circle and lands in as near a straight line as possible from the competitor. It is an art calling not only for extraordinary strength, but also canny balance and timing.

Unsung heroes

Today, many of the athletes are professionals and it is for this reason that the impressive performances do not find their way into the record books. This is especially true of track events; times set by competitors in sprint events have often approached Olympic standards. Ricky Dunbar, an Edinburgh sprinter, for example, dashed off 100 yards in 9.6 seconds, and the 100 metres has been clocked in 11.0 seconds. For the past twenty years, however, 'Big Bill' Anderson, a Grampian 'superman', has dominated the Highland Games circuit.

Competitors in light events wear conventional running kit but this was not always so. Who of the spectators watching a certain Peter Cameron will forget the day this daring young man achieved a high jump of 5ft 7in *wearing a kilt*?

More than muscle

But Highland Gatherings have always been more than just an opportunity to display physical fitness. Piping and dancing – important aspects of the martial tradition – were also popular. So much so that at various times laws were passed to prohibit them – archery and swordplay were considered of more importance in the interest of national defence. In the 1870s, however (following the lifting of the ban on the wearing of the tartan, imposed by the victorious British after the defeat of the Jacobite cause at Culloden in 1746), many people thought it important to encourage these aspects of Scottish culture. Thus they once again became a prominent feature of the Games.

The *piobaireachd* (pronounced peebroch) is the centuries-old classical music of the bagpipes, and prizes in piping are highly coveted. As well as slow-time strathspeys and jaunty jigs and reels, marches are also represented for the pipes were considered an instrument of war as well as peace. Certainly a lot of Sassenachs consider them frightful.

No one holidaymaking in the Highlands from June to September could dare admit to not having visited one of the colourful and thrilling Games – probably the most soul-stirring and picturesque sights in the world – with their uniquely Scottish, indeed Highland, individuality.

*A*thletic competitions have a long history in Scotland. There is a tradition that King Malcolm III, as long ago as the 11th century, held a contest in the Braes of Mar to find his fastest runners and toughest fighting men.

The modern Braemar Highland Gathering, under royal patronage since the days of Queen Victoria, is one of the great events of the Highland year. There are other Highland Games, too. Some, notably at Aboyne, are famous for their dancing events, others, such as those at Ballater, for 'heavy' events to demonstrate male prowess: putting the shot, throwing the hammer and tossing the caber. In neighbouring Strathdon, the older Lonach Games feature a splendid March of the Clansmen round the mansion houses of the valley.

Community affairs

In many parts of Scotland the gatherings had their beginnings in purely social events, such as weddings, where the celebrations would include challenges of one type or another, and where the whole community would become involved. A lot of the events seen today developed from the simple amusements of local workers. High- and long-jumping and running events (some of them up

Working in the Top Country

'*The top country*' is what the Highlands and Islands Development Board calls its particular patch of Britain. This is a clever name because it is at the top of the map that the patch lies, and it suggests to the industrialists and the developers, at which it is aimed, that the country is at the head of the league for everything that the visitor or the entrepreneur may desire. And yet the very existence of a '*development board*' suggests that this is a land with problems – a land of promise where the milk and honey has yet to be made to flow. Whether they ever will is the planners' problem; but whether their flowing would be to the benefit of one of the most unspoilt parts of Britain is a moral-philosophical problem of the kind that is hardest to solve. '*Bring in industry but don't touch the scenery*', was the cry that went up to the founding fathers of the Highland Board, and the balancing of these two irreconcilables is one of the embarrassments that will become more acute if recession begins to bite less.

Strength and weakness

The real dilemma of the Scottish Northlands is that their greatest strength is seen to be their greatest weakness. The Highlands represent one sixth of the total land area of the United Kingdom but they contain only 350,000 people – the equivalent of the joint populations of the London boroughs of Camden and Islington – and a sparse population, in a spectacular but intractable countryside, will always find it difficult to generate the wealth to sustain an increasing demand for amenity and convenience. Thus, that 'greatest strength' of a wild and beautiful land has created what has become known over the years as 'the Highland problem'. There is a lot of elbowroom in the Highlands and some unsuspecting visitors (a better word than tourists) who rush there unforewarned in the summer may be forgiven for thinking that what the Highlander regards as God's own country is in fact, God-foresaken.

But those who think the latter way are the ones who should go to Marbella or Majorca where the beaches are roasting and raucous and the transistors sustain a safety line with home; the empty Highlands are for those who want to breathe unpolluted air, smell the indefinable quality of wind from sea and heather, and gaze on land which varies from the overwhelming mountains of Glencoe to the lonely white beaches of Sutherland.

Fortunately for the Highlands there are thousands who still prefer freedom to funfair, because tourism is probably the largest single industry of the area and, thankfully, it is being promoted in a way which has allayed the old fear that it would turn the native population into 'a nation of waiters'.

After Culloden

The whole of Highland history pivoted in 1745 when most of the Highland clans rose with Charles Edward Stuart (Bonnie Prince Charlie) in a last desperate attempt to wrest the British Crown back from the Hanovarian dynasty. The attempt ended in disaster. The revenge of the British Government was terrible and in many cases, the former clan lands were given over to Lowland

Every Scottish clan has its own colourful tartan, each one different in some respect from all the others

sheep farmers who over-ran the best countryside with Cheviot sheep. Hundreds of thousands of these Highland displaced persons emigrated to the colonies and the cities which began to be spawned in the Lowlands by the Industrial Revolution. Thus was created the empty sixth of Great Britain.

A land of all seasons

Highlanders live happily with their seasonal visitors; many live well by them. In a reasonably good year, for example, two million visitors can be expected to trek the Highland trail and spend something in the region of £250 million. The figures, however, cannot be projected to go on increasing in any pre-ordained fashion because one summer of torrential rain can have a disastrous effect on its successor and wipe out the invaluable word-of-mouth publicity (the most important of all) that two glorious summers in a row may have generated; for, despite the superb winter sports facilities of the Cairngorms and Glencoe, the Highland tourist trade will, inevitably, remain overwhelmingly a trade of summer. A pity for the visitor, because spring and late autumn in the north have an enchantment of beauty. But perhaps it isn't such a pity for those on the other side of the counter (as opposed to the other side of the till!) because it may be the very seasonal nature of the business that has averted the old Highlander's dread vision of the 'nation of waiters'. One of the first things that one notices in even the most sophisticated Highlands hotels and restaurants (and the sophistication is seeping steadily into the perceptions of the guides to good living) is the absence of tail-coated waiters and the preponderance of charming, Highland girls who serve without subservience. They are frequently wives and mothers making a valuable contribution to the family budget.

A host of friends
Despite the proliferation of excellent hotels and guesthouses, perhaps the best way of seeing the Highlands is by the bed and breakfast networks. Not the motel type of thing, but the Highland home in which a bedroom and breakfast are provided for extraordinarily modest charges. It is a superb method of feeling (as opposed to just seeing) the life of the country. In such places one invariably gets the feeling of being a visitor to friends, and the exchange of money is made to feel incidental.

The system operates two ways; many home-owners who tiptoe into the bed and breakfast business make friends for life and claim that they would remain in the business even if financial considerations made it unnecessary, just because of the fascination of daily meeting unexpected people from other places.

Apart from the quantifiable values of tourism, one of the great advantages of the trade, as it is presently conducted, is that it meets that criterion of an industry which 'doesn't touch the scenery'. But the greatest advantage of all is that it slots into what is, undoubtedly, the most important way of working and living in the Scottish Highlands, and that is agriculture.

If one were to go by published figures, one would certainly boggle at such a claim for agriculture because the Highland Board's own figures show only 5200 people (or 4.3%) of the population to be employed in it. But, as with so many other aspects of Highland life, the agricultural system is difficult to explain – one has to go back to that pivotal year of Culloden to find the roots of understanding.

From kelp to croft
Despite the huge numbers who emigrated as a result of the wholesale introduction of sheep-farming there still remained (mainly on the coasts) a vast residue of people bereft of their partriarchial leadership but still employable as cheap labour in the kelp trade. This harvesting of wet seaweed for the production of iodine, glass, rudimentary cosmetics and a hundred other end-products made fortunes for the entrepreneurs, just as the huge new sheep-runs were making fortunes for their owners. The kelpers worked under conditions which Harriet Beecher Stowe described as being worse than the plight of the negro slaves in America.

The real tragedy came, however, when the final collapse of the kelp industry came with the end of the Napoleonic Wars (which re-opened the kelp-related European markets) and the catacyclismic

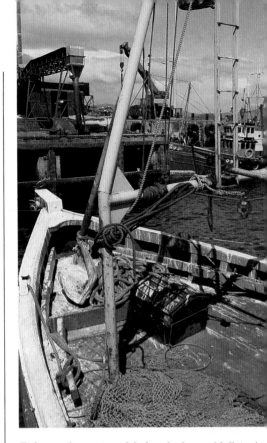

Fisherman's-eye view of the busy harbour at Mallaig

potato famine of 1846. Many of those who didn't die were assisted by the Government to resume the emigration exodus; the unfortunate ones were left as the stub-end of a demoralised and redundant population, still congested in uncongenial surroundings. Slowly a new leadership emerged, and a cry went up for land. The cry became a demand. And the demand became a crusade. Ultimately, towards the end of the 19th century, various reluctant acts of Government resulted in the breaking up of successive large private estates into small-holdings which were rented out at modest rents to individuals and their descendants in perpetuity. This is what we call today the crofting system – a system guarded in the Highlands with a zeal which is almost hallowed. A croft is a piece of land which can range from two acres to, perhaps, thirty acres in size and, in addition, a crofting township has access to substantial tracts of communal grazing for its stock. Only a minuscular number of crofters have taken advantage of a recent law which would allow them to buy their crofts, choosing, rather, to live in the security of their tenure and retaining their rights to various grants and subsidies and building loans.

Put that way it sounds like an idyllic way of life and, in some ways, it may be; but it is not a way of livelihood since few, if any, crofters can survive without a wage-earning job of some kind. Since the 12,300 crofters are classed as self-employed they do not appear among the 4.3% catalogued as being employed in Highland agriculture, although they form far and away the most important of the three agricultural strands of functioning estates (as opposed to sporting ones), hill farms and smallholdings.

Cottage crafts
Spin-offs from tourism are becoming increasingly important in the pattern of working in the Highlands. With encouragement from the Highland Board and the Scottish Tourist Board

Gairloch fishing fleet about to weigh anchor. In contrast (left), Aberdeen's Victoria Docks in 1885

high quality craft work is becoming an increasingly important part of the Highland economy. And appropriately so since it is a natural extension of indigenous cottage occupations like knitting and weaving.

Craft work fits well as that 'subsidiary industry' which is all-important to the crofter and desirable for the smaller hill farming households, but it also offers opportunities as full-time occupations for people prepared to invest minimal capital, but much dedication, taste and expertise. The Harris Tweed industry which is the most internationally renowned of all the Highland cottage crafts is, of course, by law confined to the Outer Hebrides, but the weaving of other tweeds and checks and tartans is being progressed with ever-increasing attention to style and design. (So far as tartan is concerned individual designs are pre-ordained, anyway). Where woven textiles are concerned, weaving is, for the most part, concentrated on small local factories such as Highland Tweeds in Dingwall or Thomas and Leslie in the little village of Fearnmore in Wester Ross. Such businesses tend to be family owned. There is a school of thought which advocates co-operatively owned factories in which, for example, a crofter could work his own chosen hours during bad weather or slack seasons on the croft.

Until recently there has been a resistance to local co-operatives in the Highlands but there is now a discernible move towards marketing co-operatives in an effort to reduce the high cost of living (probably the highest in the United Kingdom) fuelled by the high cost of transport. The transport factor is less significant when local crafts sales can be targeted at the migratory tourist trade; consequently smaller artefacts like leather goods, knitwear, silverware, pottery – practically all of exceedingly high standard – tend to make more and more contribution to the local economy. There was a time when the manufacture of the Highland souvenir product tended to be the provenance of the 'white settler' – the derogatory term for the escapee from the city hoping to make a quaint living in a quaint land – but the persistent efforts of the various development agencies are beginning to give credibility to the craft industries, and a reputation for quality and authenticity which is beginning to banish the tartan dancing doll with the hidden label saying 'made in Japan'.

Persistent organisation and quality control are also beginning to counter the disadvantages of dependence on tourist trade alone. Highland Craftpoint in Beauly offers not only high quality instruction courses for local craftsmen but is also funded to expand the trade into international export markets. In 1985, Craftpoint's trade development centre displayed the work of 170 craft producers to buyers from over the world; they included buyers from Saks, Gimbels and Macys from New York, and one buyer from Boston who thought it worth her while to fly over from America for one day; she placed orders with twelve companies. Small is now not only proving to be beautiful but also profitable from the point of view of the Highlander working in the Highlands.

Copper stills in the Glenfiddich whisky distillery

Net results

The degraded people of almost two centuries ago huddled on a shore-line, of which they had no knowledge, to eke out a living by fishing in which they had no expertise. But they developed it. And the men cleared from the rich straths and glens of Caithness and Sutherland evolved into one of the hardiest tribes of fishermen in the world. Like the crofters, they did get help when it was almost too late, and, at the end of the 18th century the British Fisheries Society built fishing towns (some of them among the most picturesque in the Highlands) like Tobermory in Mull, and Ullapool in Wester Ross. They prospered while fishing was a hard struggle between men with their wits and the seas with their whims, but, in the face of new technologies which swept and scraped the inner seas with scant regard to conservation, Highland fishing declined as it did throughout the rest of the British Isles.

The Highlanders (less than many), however, were unable to invest in expensive powerful boats that could penetrate the grim but rich waters of Greenland and Iceland while these were still in the public domain. Consequently they were the first to suffer hardship when the inshore fishing grounds were virtually vacuumed clean. Once more the remoteness from the markets militated against them. Now, within the constrictions of EEC policy, the Highland Board is injecting vast sums of money into modernising and underpinning the fishing business and its ancillaries. In certain areas the Board's efforts have met with considerable success with fish landings in the Highland area (although the figures include the Western Isles) rising in 1984, for example, by 55,000 tonnes to represent 60% of the total Scottish catch.

But, for the fisherman working in the Highlands, those figures aren't quite as promising as they look; in terms of men employed in the industry the latest available figures show the number of men living by catching fish to have dropped to a new low figure of 2800; in Highland fishing, as in so many areas of British life, technology is rapidly reducing the ratio of working men to the quantity of product that they produce. Consequently the Highlander living by fishing has to adapt himself to aspects of his trade wherein the new technologies can be manipulated in his favour, and more and more men are seeking to make their livings by farming the sea instead of harvesting it.

Wild fish farming, salmon and trout farming, mussel and oyster farming are now booming trades that were virtually unknown in the north a quarter of a century ago. Traditional inshore fishermen have been heard to complain that they can't sink their nets and lobster pots in the sheltered lochs of the west Highlands for all the fish cages and mussel rafts!

Industries old and new

Man's ways of working in the Highlands are changing, and changing rapidly, except in a few of the older time-honoured trades where change is quite likely to be bad for the product. Changing tastes and the eternal quest for the exotic may be denting the profits of the whisky industry, but the stills of the Spey Valley dare not be computerised or re-built in fancy alloys lest the spirit loses its soul. But the whisky industry was never a labour-intensive one and its fluctuations tend to affect balance sheets rather than employment figures.

Old trades have been revived to give nature a helping hand – not always the primary pre-occupation of modern man. When Doctor Johnson made his celebrated journey of his less than thirty years after Culloden one of his persistent grumbles was that there were no trees. Today, most of the Highland hillsides are forested up to the snow-line and close on three thousand men work for the Forestry Commission. Factories and yards have sprung up on the east coast to service the North Sea oilfields and, so far, they have not succeeded in materialising the fear of 'spoiling the scenery'; nor have they materially affected the Highland unemployment figure which remains obdurately around the 14% mark. But, in this part of the country, less than any other, one is less aware of the ravages of unemployment – probably because the quality of life is good and because those glens and mountain-sides have been empty for so long.

Hutton oil-drilling platform in Cromerty Firth

Staying Alive

A personal view on self-preservation in the wilds by author and journalist HAMISH BROWN *– a specialist in long-distance walking and orienteering, who has learnt the hard way . . .*

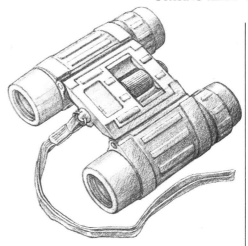

Well worth the climb: Loch Avon in the Cairngorms

*T*here is a peninsula in Western Scotland which is almost an island and it feels even more insular because the narrow landward approach is moated by a notorious stream. Normally one can boulder-hop across this 'wee Highland burn' in a few strides, but there was one rainy occasion when I was trapped and had to wait 24 hours for the spate to subside.

On another occasion I visited a crossing and the current knocked me over so I was pinned below the water by my rucksack. It was a nasty experience, but tragedy overtook one of my best friends at that crossing. He pushed on when he should have waited and the river simply swept him away to dump his body in the sea a mile down the hill. As the French say: 'Experience is the sum of near misses'.

While going into the great outdoors in no more dangerous than motoring off on any other holiday, it does have its own techniques of survival.

Weather – the unpredictable factor
The biggest single factor dominating outdoor activities is the weather. Rain, an inconvenience at home, or welcomed by gardeners, can create desperate hazards, as I've mentioned. Ben Nevis, at 4416ft, is Britain's highest mountain and therefore a lure to adventurers of all ages and skills. It kills more people than does the Eiger and many of them are simply walking up the tourist track. The trouble is that it may be a warm, sunny day at Fort William, but up there a gale may be driving sleet or rain on the scantily-clad visitor. It is a question of knowing the dangers and being equipped to meet them.

When I began my wanderings as a boy I made plenty of mistakes and had my share of hammerings, but this did not curtail enjoyment or dampen enthusiasm – even when soaked to the skin. I actually weighed up clothes after one soaking and then again after I'd dried everything. The difference was 10 lb: a gallon of water! Given a bitter wind that day I would probably have ended up a hypothermia case. That word had not been invented then, of course, neither had vibram soles or nylon outer garments.

Quite a few practicalities can be looked at almost in a mechanical way. A car needs fuel and servicing and so do those going into wild country. Even the easiest walking burns up calories so top up with a sandwich or a bar of chocolate; fresh air makes for gnawing appetites, a clear indication of the refreshing goodness of the outdoors. I love my car, but only because it takes me to the places where I can explore on foot.

Read all about it
It is worthwhile buying or borrowing books about this pursuit. The great outdoors has a tremendous literature and there are monthly magazines for every taste.

Scotland is a wonderful country for enjoying the wilds. After a boyhood spent under the Ochil hills and wanderings in mountain ranges all round the world I appreciate it more and more. There are just two drawbacks: the weather, which can be unreliable and the midges, which can be diabolical. These, alas, mostly coincide with statutory summer holidays, while May and June are more reliable and October is enhanced by the rich colours of autumn. Winter can often give some of the most splendid days of all, but there is a heightening of all the usual dangers and the introduction of new hazards to accompany the snow. Walking stick gives way to ice axe.

Self-preservation
In some ways I feel too much fuss is made of dangers and difficulties. Most of my early days, summer and winter, were spent in solitary wanderings in the Ochils and I did not come to grief despite some escapades. I was there because of my own enthusiasm, and the 'fierce joy of living' is both a driving force and a safeguard. When you love living you take care to preserve life. Man is a naturally cautious animal so when difficulties or dangers loom he takes measures to cope. Sometimes this may call for a retreat, but it could mean trying to cope with a situation and learning from the new experience. A child knows fire burns only when he touches it, not because of endless

maternal warnings. So, if you have a hankering to move off the beaten track, then go. Remember though, that distances can be deceptive and you need the stamina to cope with a return journey.

Going alone is always condemned yet is an essential element. It is the only way to learn real self-sufficiency and confidence in one's own abilities. If there are others with you there is an element of lazy reliance on them. I always smile when I remember the story of how Chris Bonington and other top climbers floundered, lost on Creag Mheagaidh, because each had assumed that the others would have map and compass and so had not bothered to take these essentials. Any one of them, going alone, would naturally have taken them. Going alone is, in fact, safer because the solitary adventurer proceeds with heightened consciousness and efficiency. I dislike 'rules' that give categorical do's and don'ts. The wild can always produce situations not covered by rules, so the programmed, rule-book walker is then both lost and shocked. An attitude of thinking out situations *all the time* is much more important than adhering to inflexible rules.

My ultimate example of this training (it is self-training as well) was in the Cairngorms when an unexpected blizzard caught us on Ben Macdhin. We could hardly move for the force of the storm and though well-equipped, things were becoming desperate. One lad struggled over to me and bellowed, face twisted by the wind: 'Is it bad enough yet to have to dig in?' Far from being frightened of a forced bivouac he was actually keen to try it. He had stayed in a snow hole already and coped with lesser storms. He had faith in himself and in me. Whatever happened he knew that there was *a best next step to take.* That is the whole key to staying alive in the great outdoors.

We didn't know it at the time, but another school party was on the same hill that day. They were weakly led and inexperienced in the Scottish hills. Exposure, aided by fear I'm sure, claimed one victim before they were rescued. The youngsters were *led* into those circumstances. If they had had any choice they would probably have gone to the Aviemore swimming pool. We go into the countryside for fun, after all, and the motivation for that must come from within the individual.

There are many centres and organisations which can assist anyone seeking outside help or company and there are scores of clubs all over the country providing friendship and fellowship. More people gain more pleasure from this pastime than any other, whether it is from simple walking or scaling the heights of Everest.

Everyone's Everest
Every May there is a coast-to-coast walking event in Scotland. This, The Ultimate Challenge, is fascinating to watch, or to participate in, because people choose their own route and go in their own style. It is not competitive. You can even go alone. On the first three years there were heatwaves, the next it rained every day of the two weeks available, and on the last two the weather has been mixed. (I've gone solo once, made three crossings with a friend, one crossing with three members of our local mountain club and one with two girls who had never done any 'serious' walking before). The numbers setting out are limited to 200 (from over 800 applicants this year) and 90% complete the course. Every year has seen people fall out from heat exhaustion – not a complaint one would expect in Scotland but a considerable menace at times. The remedy is an early start.

Whether you are just strolling for an hour on a forestry trail or walking across Scotland the basic ingredient should be fun – and that at the time rather than in retrospect. My ultimate trip was scaling all the Scottish 3000ft peaks (the Munros) in a continuous walk of 1639 miles over 112 days with 449,000ft of ascent, which is about 15 Everests. Everest need not even be a mountain. It is an outlook of life, an adventurousness at any level, in any place in the great outdoors. It is there for anyone.

A rucksack checklist
Waterproof jacket and trousers
Pullover (or equivalent)
Head and hands covering
First aid kit
Map, compass, whistle
Torch and spare batteries
Food and drink for the day
Emergency rations
Survival bag
Camera and spare rolls of film

SCOTTISH HIGHLANDS

Gazetteer

Each entry in this Gazetteer has the atlas
page number on which the place can be
found and/or its National Grid reference
included under the heading. An
explanation of how to use the National
Grid is given on page 80.

Above: Tumbling waters in the Pass of Glencoe

Aberdeen

Map Ref: 89NJ9305

Although it is the 'capital' of the North Sea oil industry, Aberdeen has many things on its municipal mind besides drilling rigs, multi-national contracts and helicopter flights to production platforms far beyond the grey horizon.

Roses, for instance – in their tens and hundreds of thousands. Aberdeen is a commercial rose-growing centre, and the 100,000 it has planted on the verges and central reservation of its main suburban bypass road help it to be a regular winner in the Britain in Bloom competition.

Appropriately enough, the most popular series produced by BBC Television in Scotland is *The Beechgrove Garden*, set in the grounds of the studio in Aberdeen's Beechgrove Terrace.

The city is lavishly supplied with public parks. Duthie Park continues the roses theme, with an entire hillside devoted to them on its site above the River Dee. Seaton Park slopes down to Aberdeen's other river, the Don. Between the two river mouths, two miles of beach have more parkland behind.

On the western outskirts, Hazelhead Park has woodland nature trails, animal and bird collections, playing fields and three of the many fine golf courses with which the city is surrounded.

In the centre of Aberdeen, Provost Skene's House and Provost Ross's House are beautifully restored 16th-century mansions; Marischal College, part of Aberdeen University, has a remarkable granite frontage – a riotous framework of intricate, ornamented pinnacles.

Between 1593 and 1860 there were two universities here. Actually, the older university – King's College – was established in the separate burgh of Old Aberdeen, but the universities, like the burghs, are long since merged.

Within easy strolling distance of King's College, where the chapel with its fine array of medieval

A corner in one of the tropical hot-houses at Aberdeen's Duthie Park

woodcarvings is regularly open to the public, are the restored 18th-century houses of Wrights' and Coopers' Place; the Chanonry where the university professors live in elegant, tree-shaded Georgian mansions; and St. Machar's Cathedral, completed early in the 16th century, with its collection of historic charters and a splendid heraldic ceiling.

AA recommends:
Hotels: Bucksburn, Moat House, Meldrum Road, Bucksburn (3m N A947), 4-star, *tel.* (0224) 713911
Caledonian Thistle, 10 Union Terrace, 3-star, *tel.* (0224) 640233
Guesthouses: For a selection of guesthouses, please consult the AA guide *Guesthouses, Farmhouses and Inns in Britain.*
Garages: Aberdeen Motors, Service Centre, 44 Union Row, *tel.* 56151
Callanders Engineering (Aberdeen), 366 King Street, *tel.* 634211
Carden Motors, Springfield Road, *tel.* 38728
Cordiners, 54 Menzies Road, *tel.* 879024 (day), 871552 (night)
Morrison Brothers, 46 Virginia Street, *tel.* 574206

Aberfeldy

Map Ref: 92NN8549

Low-set beside the sparkling waters of the Tay, Aberfeldy is best approached by the A826, the high road from the south over Glen Cochill. As the road sweeps down towards the town, the mansion houses in wooded grounds along the river valley, the farms and the open moorland summits above them, are all seen with an impressive mountain skyline beyond.

General Wade's elegant five-arched bridge over the Tay at Aberfeldy was built in 1733. Beside it stands the monument to the Black Watch regiment, erected in the town a few years later.

Off the A826 is the Birks of Aberfeldy nature trail, in the wild ravine of the Falls of Moness. 'Birks' are birches, but the trees in this mile-long glen also include beech and sycamore, oak and ash, hazel, alder and rowan.

A quiet approach often allows visitors to see roe deer browsing. Dippers and wagtails feed in the pools and by the water's edge. Finches, warblers and wood pigeons flit among the varied woodland cover.

AA recommends:
Self Catering: Aberfeldy Country Cottages, Moness Farm, *tel.* 20851
Guesthouses: Balnearn Private Hotel, Crieff Road, *tel.* 20431
Caber Feidh, 66 Dunkeld Street, *tel.* 20342
Guinach House, Urlar Road, *tel.* 20251
Nessbank House, Crieff Road, *tel.* 20214
Tom of Cluny (farmhouse), *tel.* 20477

Amid the misty Birks of Aberfeldy

Applecross

Map Ref: 86NG7144

Although its approaches are disfigured by an eyesore of an oil-platform yard, the Pass of the Cattle to Applecross remains one of the most stunning roads in Britain. After a steep but steady ascent, hairpin bends fling it to a summit at 2053ft, with an eagle's-eye view of the towering cliffs back towards Loch Kishorn.

Easier gradients take the road down across a deserted moorland with dozens of silvery hill lochs, before dipping towards the forested valley and sweeping sand bay of Applecross itself.

South of Applecross village is a coastline of sheltered inlets and rocky points, fishing and crofting hamlets. To the north, a through-road opened in the 1970s heads for the tip of Applecross peninsula. The seaward views are magnificent, across the Inner Sound to the mountain peaks of Skye, often silhouetted against the fiery splendours of a West Highland sunset.

Arbroath

Map Ref: 93NO6340

On the southern outskirts of this North Sea fishing town, the elegant white-painted building with pillared entrance and round, battlemented tower was originally the mainland signalling base for the Bell Rock lighthouse, 11 miles out to sea.

The Signal Tower is now a highly-regarded museum, with displays on subjects as varied as the Bell Rock itself, the fishing industry, the flax trade, which used to provide the basic material for sails, and the lawnmowers which have been an unexpected Arbroath speciality.

Arbroath, however, is more famous for its 'smokies', which are haddock bought by local curers at the harbour fish-auctions then smoked slowly over beechwood fires.

Its most notable building is a ruined, but carefully preserved, 12th-century abbey, with a museum explaining its considerable significance in Scottish history.

From the east end of Arbroath beach, a nature trail climbs above busy seabird colonies on a line of rugged sandstone cliffs.

AA recommends:
Guesthouse: Kingsley, 29 Market Gate, *tel.* 73933

Ardnamurchan

Map Ref: 90NM4167

This is the most westerly parish on the British mainland. From the lighthouse on Ardnamurchan Point there is a breathtaking view of open sea and islands: Coll and Tiree; the Small Isles of Rum, Eigg and Muck; Skye and, on a clear day, the whole line of the Outer Hebrides.

The main road through Ardnamurchan is the dead-end B8007, which hugs the bays of the southern coast on its way to Kilchoan, the main village of the district. The 18th-century parish church is there, and nearby are the ruins of Mingary Castle, now an Ancient Monument but once the stronghold of the MacIans of Ardnamurchan.

Minor roads meander across the peninsula to the crofting and fishing settlements on the north coast. There are fine sandy beaches at Sanna, Portuairk, Plocaig, Achateny and Kilmory.

Much of Ardnamurchan is red deer country. Golden eagles and peregrine falcons nest, while sea-birds feed in the multitude of bays, and seals have their favourite rocks for reclining in the sun.

AA recommends:
Self Catering: The Kennels, The Cottage, Glen House, Glenborrodale, *tel.* 01-946 9779

Banchory

Map Ref: 89NO6995

At Scottish country dances all over the world, much of the foot-tapping music for jigs, reels and strathspeys was written by a Banchory man. A memorial in the High Street of this attractive Deeside town recalls Scott Skinner, the famous fiddler/composer who was born here in 1843.

Banchory is an invigorating, open-air holiday resort. There are walks in the woodlands north-west of the town; along the banks of the Dee on the edge of the well laid-out golf course; to the salmon leap at the Bridge of Feugh; and south-west of the town through bircßwoods and conifer plantations to the viewpoint summit of Scolty Hill.

Permits for salmon and sea-trout

Signal Tower at Arbroath harbour

fishing on the Dee are available in Banchory, and there are facilities for tennis, bowling, football and cricket. Visitors can also be shown round a factory whose main product is Deeside lavender.

AA recommends:
Hotel: Banchory Lodge, 3 red-star, Country House Hotel, *tel.* 2625
Self Catering: Woodend of Glassel, *tel.* 2731
Garage: Banchory Service Station, North Deeside, *tel.* 2336

Banff

Map Ref: 89NJ6863

This former county town is a showpiece of 18th-century architecture, although its history goes back to the 12th century, when it was a prosperous member of the Hanseatic trading league.

Beside the River Deveron there is a parkland golf course called Duff House Royal. It takes its name from William Adam's baroque Georgian mansion built for the 1st Earl of Fife. Duff House is unfurnished, but the fabric is maintained and it is open to the public.

Up-river, a woodland walk leads to the high-level Bridge of Alvah, built in 1772, where the Deveron spins through a rock-walled gorge.

Anglers fish the Deveron for trout and salmon, but commercial fishing-boats have mostly moved away, and Banff harbour is largely recreational.

In summer, a narrow-gauge railway, sometimes with steam-hauled trains, runs regular services from a station near the harbour to the beach at Banff Links.

AA recommends:
Guesthouses: Carmelite House Hotel, Low Street, *tel.* 2152
Ellerslie, 45 Low Street, *tel.* 5888
Garage: County (Banff Tyre Services), Carmelite Street, *tel.* 5750 (day), 2816 (night)

Sheltered Pennan harbour and the curving coast, Buchan

Bennachie

Map Ref: 89NJ6522

In view for miles around, Bennachie is one of the great hill-walking ranges of nortk-east Scotland. From the Donview Visitor Centre on the south side of the range, as well as from car parks to the east and north, a network of forest roads and footpaths climbs through plantations of spruce, pine and larch on to breezy heather moorlands. It finally peaks at the summits of Craigshannoch, Oxen Craig – at 1733ft the highest point – and the Mither Tap, one of the most striking hilltops in Scotland, defended on one side by shattered granite cliffs.

These are splendid viewpoints. In really clear weather the northerly outlook extends as far as the hills of Caithness, more than 70 miles away.

Roe deer and squirrels live in the plantations. An ancient track called the Maiden's Causeway can be traced on the north-east shoulder of the range.

AA recommends:
Self Catering: Balfluig Castle, Alford, tel. 01-242 4986
Haughton House, Haughton Country Park, Alford, tel. Alford 2107
Garage: Haughton, Montgarrie Road, Alford, tel. Alford 2331

Blair Atholl

Map Ref: 88NN8765

This is the village outside the gates of Blair Castle, home of the Duke of Atholl, chief of the Murrays. His Atholl Highlanders are the only legally recognised private army in Europe, following a privilege granted by Queen Victoria.

From the A9, the white towers of the castle rise above wooded parkland. The oldest part is Cumming's Tower, built about 1270.

More than thirty rooms are open to the public, from April to October. Most notable of them are the splendid drawing room and dining room, with white marble chimney-pieces and lavishly ornamented stucco ceilings.

There are walks and nature trails in the castle grounds. In the village itself, a working corn mill and a rural museum are open to visitors during the summer.

About three miles west of Blair Atholl is the Clan Donnaohaidh Museum at Bruar. Open from April to October, it features the history of the Robertsons, Reids and Duncans. Woodland paths and bridges lead to the nearby Falls of Bruar.

AA recommends:
Garage: Blair Atholl, tel. 221

Buchan

Map Ref: 89NJ9551

There are two separate aspects of this north-eastern corner of Scotland – the agricultural heartland and the fishing coast.

The open Buchan countryside is dotted with 'planned' 18th- a1d 19th-century villages like Cuminestown, New Byth, Mintlaw, New Pitsligo – whose restored cottages stand above commercial peat-mosses – and Stuartfield.

Turriff is a substantial red-sandstone town which hosts the biggest agricultural show in the north-east. At Aberchirder there are, unusually for Buchan, some woodland walks; the 'Foggie Show' there takes that name because almost everybody in the district calls the little town Foggieloan.

Although it is almost entirely a working landscape, Buchan has one of the finest country parks in Scotland, occupying the woodlands and riversides of the Aden estate at Old Deer. Not far away, the ruined

The Falls of Bruar, Blair Atholl

Abbey of Deer is a graceful, ancient monument in lawns set above the winding South Ugie Water.

There are few mansions or stately homes in Buchan that are regularly open to the public, but Fyvie Castle is now owned by the National Trust for Scotland and is expected to be opened in 1986.

Buchan fishermen's multi-million pound investment in deep-sea fishing boats and the most modern equipment has made Peterhead the biggest white-fish port in Western Europe. When midnight strikes on Sunday, there is a magnificent show as upwards of 300 illuminated boats – including North Sea-oil support vessels – head for the open water after the obligatory day of rest.

The other main port is Fraserburgh, which boasts a two-mile beach and, like Peterhead, has an old fishertown of restored houses bypassed by the modern bustle.

Buchan also has many attractively-placed fishing villages of an older, far less industrialised, style.

Gardenstown, Crovie and Pennan are the most spectacularly located, at the foot of seabird cliffs topped by exhilarating headland walks.

Castles of Mar

Map Ref: 89NJ4807

While there are many sturdy fortresses in the old province of Mar, between the upper valleys of the Dee and the Don, the castles in the care of the National Trust for Scotland were intended less as strongholds and more as grandly-designed and opulently-furnished private homes.

Craigievar Castle, in the hills south of Alford, was completed in 1626 by the Bell family of architects and masons for William Forbes, a spectacularly successful Aberdeen merchant in the Baltic trade who was known as 'Danzig Willie'.

This is the classic fairytale castle, whose plain lower floors gradually blossom out into elegantly rounded upper towers and turrets and a rooftop viewing balcony. It is notable for its moulded plaster ceilings, oak panelling and elegant hall complete with musician's gallery.

The Bells were also involved in the building of Crathes Castle near Banchory, although the Burnett lairds had been landowners here for more than two and a half centuries before it was completed in 1596.

Crathes is famous for its original painted ceilings and friezes. Outside, there are eight linked gardens deliberately varied in style and colours, with massive yew hedges planted in 1702.

Farther afield in the 595-acre estate, nature trails wander through varied woodland and open farming country, past ponds and meandering burns.

About 10 miles north of Crathes, the Bells followed an earlier family of inspired masons – the Leipers – in the task of creating another masterpiece at Castle Fraser, finished in 1636.

AA recommends:
Hotel: Banchory, 3 red-star Country House Hotel, *tel.* Banchory 2625
Self Catering: Balfluig Castle, Alford, *tel.* 01-242 4986
Haughton House, Haughton Country Park, Alford, *tel.* 2107
Woodend of Glassel, Banchory, *tel.* 2731
Garage: Banchory Service Station, North Deeside Banchory, *tel.* 2336

Crathes Castle, completed in 1596, has eight linked gardens with massive yews

Comrie

Map Ref: 92NN7722

Lying exactly on the Highland Boundary Fault, this 18th-century 'planned village', where the River Lednock and the Water of Ruchill meet the River Earn, was once so prone to earth tremors that an Earthquake House was built. It is still standing, and contains illustrations of some of the Victorian earthquake-recording devices. Pegs falling over on the flat earth floor showed the strength and direction of each shock. Although the worst of the tremors were over 100 years ago, many people in the village have tales of dishes suddenly rattling in their cupboards.

'Comrie Fortnight' every summer features parades, music, guided walks and sporting events. On 31 December, the Old Year is seen out with a torchlight procession.

Trout fishing is available on the Earn. There is an attractive golf course, and Comrie has an old-established village cricket club.

The Circular Walk in Glen Lednock passes two fine waterfalls on its way through natural woodland, open farmland and forestry plantations. A very steep path off the Glen Lednock road leads to the –nest viewpoint in the district, beside the Melville Monument on the summit of Dunmore.

Comrie is the home of the Museum of Scottish Tartans, which has displays on individual patterns, the history of Highland dress and a sample of the tartan which reached the moon.

AA recommends:
Guesthouses: Mossgiel, *tel.* 70567
West Ballindaloch (farmhouse), Glenlednock, *tel.* 70282
Garage: T A Douglas, Burrell Street, *tel.* 70241

Cowal

Map Ref: 91NS0587

Surrounded and deeply indented by sea-lochs, with forested hillsides and magnificent walks, sailing centres and haunts of anglers, famous gardens and an abiding sense of history, Cowal is a Highlands in miniature.

The most direct way into Cowal is by car ferry across the Firth of Clyde

Comrie from the bridge looking to Melville Monument

to Dunoon or Hunter's Quay. But the most scenic approach is by the A83 from Arrochar. It runs through the mountainous northern fringes of the 100 square-mile Argyll Forest Park, over the Rest and be Thankful, an 860ft pass where the line of the old military road of 1750 is used today for motorsport events.

Beyond the summit, the A83 carries on past the dark waters of Loch Restil, reflecting the crags and rocky ledges of Beinn an Lochain towering above. Then it sweeps down through Glen Kinglas to the junction where the A815 turns left into the heart of Cowal.

Soon, the B839 comes in from the east, through the forbiddingly named Hell's Glen, with its claustrophobic hillsides. Over that way, and also reached by the B828 Glen Mhor road which turns off just after the summit of Rest and be Thankful, is Lochgoilhead.

This holiday village at the head of the fjord-like Loch Goil is a centre for hill-walking, pony-trekking, sea-angling, sailing, and water-skiing.

Back on the A815, the main road heads for the villages of St. Catherines and Strachur, both with hotels overlooking Loch Fyne. At Strachur the A815 turns inland, to its most impressive, winding stretch along the eastern shore of Loch Eck, a favourite watersports area.

Beyond the foot of Loch Eck is the Younger Botanic Garden, open from April to October. The main approach is an avenue of soft-barked Wellingtonias, but the finest feature of the garden's 120 acres is the brilliant display of more than 250 species of rhododendrons, at their most colourful in the late spring and early summer. On the other side of the A815 from the Wellingtonia avenue, footpaths lead up into a network of hill and forest walks, notably the splendidly wooded Puck's Glen.

The A815 approaches the sea on the outskirts of Kilmun on the Holy Loch, where the view is ruined by the dull grey outlines of the US Navy's Polaris submarine base.

Heading in the direction of Dunoon, the A815 comes to Sandbank, where several America's Cup yachts were built. A coast road goes past Lazaretto Point, once the site of a quarantine station, by

Hunter's Quay and Kirn. The shorter inland road reaches Dunoon direct by Loch Loskin.

Dunoon has been a holiday resort since Victorian times. There are bowling greens and an 18-hole golf course with wide-ranging views over the Firth of Clyde, walks and trout-stocked reservoirs, sailing and sea-angling. The Cowal Highland Gathering, held every August at Dunoon, is a hectic weekend of piping competitions, Highland dancing and athletics.

South of Dunoon the A815 passes through another resort at Innellan, where Florence Nightingale spent many holidays, past Toward Point and the lighthouse on a loop road at its tip, to finish at Port Lamont on Loch Striven. But Port Lamont, named after the family who were once the most powerful clan chiefs in the district, is not the end of the public road.

Turning right, a pleasant shore road passes the lonely parish church of Inverchaolin, where many of the Lamonts are buried. Several oil tankers and cargo ships are laid up, for want of business, in the deep and sheltered waters of this faraway Highland sea-loch.

The motorist's way to the head of Loch Striven is back through Dunoon and Sandbank, then off the A815 on to the B836, a narrower and winding road across a much wilder landscape. Clachaig, the only village along it, has a scattered look: the Clyde Gunpowder Mills were built here in Napoleonic times, and it was advisable to keep the buildings well apart.

On the far side of the peninsula between Loch Striven and Loch Riddon, the B836 meets the newly rebuilt A886. The left turn here follows the winding shore of Loch Riddon to the strung-out village of Colintraive, from which a car ferry sails to Rhubodach at the north end of the Island of Bute. Beyond Colintraive a narrow road comes to an end beside those marine 'white elephants' moored in Loch Striven.

Travelling back from Colintraive, past the end of the B836, leads to a road junction at the foot of Glendaruel. The A886 continues up the glen, alongside the trout and salmon waters of the River Ruel, on the shortest way back to Strachur.

But the turn to the south, on to the A8003 which was opened in 1969, leads towards some of the most spectacular viewpoints in Scotland, as it climbs high above the coastline then dips down again to Tighnabruaich on the western arm of the Kyles of Bute, the narrow strait which separates the Island of Bute from the mainland.

Tighnabruaich – Gaelic for 'the house on the hillside' – grew up in Victorian times when a steamer pier was built to tap the Clyde coasts holiday traffic. Today it is the yachting centre of the Kyles of Bute. South of Tighnabruich is Kames.

More forest walks and picnic areas have been laid out beside the loop road towards Ardlamont Point and back to Millhouse, on the B8000 west of Kames. Millhouse used to be the site of another gunpowder factory, supplied with water from two reservoirs to the north. Still known as the Powder Dams, they are stocked with trout and link up with one of the tougher hill-walking routes.

North of Millhouse, the B8000 runs inland through Kilfinan to Otter Ferry, back on Loch Fyne. There was once a ferry here, but 'Otter' is a corruption of the Gaelic *oitir* – a sandy spit which can be seen stretching well out into the loch at low tide.

Last of the little villages of Cowal, as this circular tour links up again with the A886 near Strachur, is Newton. Tucked away on the shore of Loch Fyne, Newton offers many of the traditional attractions of Cowal – peace and quiet, and views over a beautiful loch to the wooded hills.

Crieff

Map Ref: 92NN8621

The location of this old-established market town, where the Highlands sweep up from the gentle plain of Strathearn, not only made it a famous

Crieff golf club with the woods and heathland of Knock Hill in the background

The wild morainic landscape of the forbiddingly-named Hell's Glen in Cowal

cattle-trading centre in the 18th century, but also brought it many misadventures during the Jacobite Risings.

Crieff is on a steeply sloping site above the River Earn. At the highest level, Strathearn Hydro is a Victorian hotel in extensive grounds, established to take advantage of the pure waters of the Turret Burn. These are also supplied to the Glenturret distillery, which dates from 1775.

There are visitors tours of the distillery, as well as of Crieff's more recently founded pottery, paperweight, glass and crystal factories.

Above the Hydro, pathways lead on to the woods and heathland of the Knock. There is a nature trail at Culcrieff on the west side. Crieff golf club covers undulating land towards the east.

About 4 miles south-east of Crieff, along the B8062, is the 17th-century Innerpeffray library, which is still open every day except Thursdays, and has a notable collection of bibles.

Close to the basin on the Crinan canal

Crinan

Map Ref: 90NR7894

A favourite port of call for yachts on their way to and from the cruising grounds of the Western Isles, this small but busy and colourful place marks the seaward end of the Crinan Canal, opened in 1801 to cut out the often hazardous voyage round the Mull of Kintyre.

From Ardrishaig on Loch Fyne, the canal arrives at Crinan with thickly wooded hillsides on its south bank and an embankment with tow-path separating it from the sea-loch to the north. Yachts and fishing boats mingle in the basin, and the seafood restaurant in the hotel overlooking a wild and rocky coastline is a two-minute stroll from where the catches are landed.

Oddly enough, Crinan Harbour is a different place nearby. A network of forest walks starts there, leading most notably to a superb viewpoint across the sound to the mountainous islands of Jura and Scarba. Between them is the fearsome whirlpool of Corryvreckan, whose roaring tide-race can be heard at Crinan on a still day.

The area between Crinan and Kilmartin contains many well-preserved standing stones, and the ancient hilltop fort of Dunadd was the capital of the kings of Dalriada.

AA recommends:
Hotel: Crinan, 3-star, *tel.* 235
Self Catering: Kilmahamaig Barns, *tel.* 238

Cruden Bay

Map Ref: 89NK0936

More than a mile of excellent curving beach here is backed by grassy dunes which themselves give way to a pair of naturally-landscaped golf courses. From 1899 the luxury Cruden Bay Hotel was a top people's social and sporting resort, but it was dismantled after the second world war.

North of the sands, reached by a road past the restored cottages of Port Erroll, the little Water of Cruden – diverted in 1798 – runs into a once-busy fishing harbour. Nets are still dried on the traditional poles, but the fishing is much reduced and the harbour is also used by weekend sailors.

The original course of the river reaches the sea below the cliffs where the ruins of Slains Castle stand ragged against the sky. They are said to have given author Bram Stoker, a regular holidaymaker at Cruden Bay, the idea for Count Dracula's castle.

AA recommends:
Garage: Bayview, South Road, Peterhead, *tel.* 5171 (day), 77326 (night)

Dornoch

Map Ref: 85NH7989

This graceful little town beside the Dornoch Firth was once a cathedral city. A Bishop of Caithness had the cathedral built in the 13th century. Although it was sacked by the Reformers in 1570, it was later rebuilt and is now the parish church.

More grimly, a memorial stone in a town garden marks the place where Janet Horn, the last woman to be executed in Scotland for witchcraft, was burned at the stake in 1722.

Around Dornoch there are miles of safe, sandy beaches. And the splendidly kept Old Course of Royal Dornoch Golf Club offers, in the opinion of many experts, the most northerly first-class golf in the world.

AA recommends:
Self Catering: Pitgrudy Farm Holidays, Pitgrudy Farm, *tel.* 810291

Sacked in 1570 then rebuilt, Dornoch Cathedral is now the parish church

A Highland chief in Stuart tartan

Tartan

There is a charming legend that tartan was first mentioned in the Old Testament when Joseph wore his coat of many colours. Regrettably it isn't true because the word tartan comes from the French word *tartaine*, a particular kind of French cloth which has nothing to do with colour at all. If Joseph has spoken Gaelic then he would call his Technicolor dream coat *breacan*, which is the Gaelic for a multi-coloured cloth.

The idea does go back a long way. Virgil, half a century before Christ, made reference to 'striped and shiny coats' which is much nearer to the striped linen shirt that the invading Irish introduced to Scotland in the 7th century. It is from these striped shirts that *breacan* (or tartan as we now know it) has descended and, over the years, it became a criss-crossed with coloured threads to give a recognisable tartan by the end of the 16th century.

In those days, tartans tended to identify the territorial area in which a man lived, and since families of the same name tended to congregate in the same straths and glens, the particular area tartan became associated with that particular family or clan name.

Today there are almost two hundred tartans, each one clearly attached to a clan. Legally there is nothing to stop anyone wearing anyone else's tartan although it is highly unlikely that, after years of bitter strife, a Macdonald would be seen alive in a Campbell tartan even if he might be happy to marry a Campbell wife. What is zealously guarded is the word 'tartan'; in courtesy at least, a new tartan (as opposed to a check) has to be approved by the Scottish Lyon King at Arms and by the Standing Council of Scottish Chiefs. But so far nobody has been sent to the Tower (or even to the dungeons of Edinburgh Castle) for flaunting what is, after all, a charming and romantic tradition. With so many official tartans to choose from the chances are that, with a little research, everyone can find one to which he or she can lay even tenuous kinship claim!

Dufftown

Map Ref: 88NJ3240

In 1817 James Duff, the 4th Earl of Fife, began to lease building plots in the town that took his name. Only six years later, Mortlach Distillery opened on the banks of the Dullan Water.

Now there are seven malt whisky distilleries in the town. One of the main attractions is the supply of peaty water, from the Dullan and the Fiddich, Jock's Well and the Priest's Well. Visitors are given guided tours, on weekdays, of Glenfiddich Distillery, which is also the start of a motoring Malt Whisky Trail (see page 63).

Pleasant walks around Dufftown include one to Mortlach church, on a site used for worship since 566, then up the wooded banks of the Dullan past the Linen Apron waterfall.

AA recommends:
Self Catering: Gordon & Richmond Cottages, Tullochallum, *tel.* Kennethmont 250

Dunkeld

Map Ref: 92NO0242

Steeply wooded crags overlooking a double bend on the Tay give Dunkeld a dramatic riverside setting. Above the river stands the ruined medieval cathedral, sacked by the Reformers in 1560 but partly restored. The 13th-century choir is now the parish church.

In 1689 most of Dunkeld was burned to the ground in the aftermath of the Battle of Killiecrankie. Many of the replacement town-centre houses of that period have been beautifully restored. A National Trust for Scotland information centre describes the work involved.

Linked to Dunkeld by a Telford bridge of 1809 is the Victorian village of Birnam. Beatrix Potter's tales of Peter Rabbit and Mr Jeremy Fisher the Frog were written on successive days while she was on holiday at the house called Eastwood, across the Tay from Birnam's riverbank Terrace Walk.

The Tay near here is a famous salmon river, and Dunkeld is an excellent centre for walking. From the A9, just west of the town, a woodland trail goes to the Hermitage, a summer-house of 1758

Dunkeld bridge over the River Tay

beside the Falls of the Braan. There are several Forestry Commission walks around the village of Inver, on the high ground of Craigvinean Forest.

AA recommends:
Hotel: Dunkeld House, 3-star, Country House Hotel, tel. 771

Durness

Map Ref: 84NC4067

Standing back from a rugged coast where cliff-faces dip down to sandy coves, and sea-bird colonies far outnumber human settlements, Durness is surrounded by well-tended crofting fields. East of the village is Smoo Cave, the most famous feature in this limestone landscape. Visitors can approach by boat, but detailed exploration is for experienced potholers only.

To the north-west is Faraid Head at the tip of the hilly peninsula. The road to it passes Balnakeil, where there is a craft village, a ruined church of 1619 and a fine west-facing beach backed by sheltering dunes.

At Keoldale on the Kyle of Durness a passenger ferry links up with the May-September minibus service over the wild country of the Parph, where eagles nest and gannets fly the offshore air currents to Cape Wrath. The lighthouse there, built in 1827 on top of 400ft cliffs, marks the

remote north-western corner of mainland Britain.

Ospreys

After being lost as a breeding species since Edwardian times, ospreys — at first only one pair — began to nest again in the Highlands in the 1950s. In the early days of the re-introduction, egg-collectors ruined conservationists' attempts to safeguard the nesting sites. But the birds are now well established. Up to 20 pairs nest in the Highlands every season, in two publi-cised locations and several more which are closely guarded secrets.

The ospreys winter in West Africa and arrive in Scotland in April. Different pairs return to the RSPB reserve in the pinewoods near Loch Garten, between Aviemore and Nethy Bridge, and to the Scottish Wildlife Trust reserve at Loch of the Lowes, north-east of Dunkeld. Visitors are welcome at these sites, where close observation of the nests is possible. Other wildlife displays are mounted at both reserves.

Eggs hatch in June, and the ospreys have usually headed back towards Africa by the end of August. During the four months in between, these substantial birds of prey may be seen hunting for food in lochs near the nesting sites, swooping dramatically for fish which they snatch up in their powerful talons.

Ospreys (this is a female) now breed in several areas in the Highlands

John o' Groats

John o' Groats is a white-painted place of pilgrimage and every year quite a few people try to reach it in the shortest time on foot from Land's End. Some of them do it on roller-skates or pushing prams. Many of them believe that they are travelling from the southernmost point of Britain to the northernmost. Neither is true. Dunnet Head is the most northerly point but it has only a lighthouse to offer, while John o' Groats has a pleasant village of attractive cottages and a handful of souls, except on summer days when tourists arrive by the coach-load to take a quick glance across the Pentland Firth and a long browse through the souvenir shops. The more intrepid take advantage of the ferryboat which sails at regular intervals across the spectacular Pentland Firth to South Ronaldsay in Orkney, passing on the way the lonely little island of Stroma inhabited by only a handful of people but a host of sea-birds. Is the ferryman a descendant of his predecessor of long ago — John de Groot, who came to Scotland from Holland and became the ferryman in the village to which he gave his name? There is a good hotel for those wishing to enjoy the purest, clearest air to be found anywhere in the country.

Elgin

Map Ref: 88NJ2162

As the old county town of Moray, Elgin retains many graceful buildings. Most famous of them is the ruined 13th-century cathedral known as the Lanthorn (Lantern) of the North. It is regarded as the finest of all Scottish cathedrals in design.

About 4 miles south-west of the town, the picnic site at Torrieston is the starting point of a network of trails in the hills of Monaughty Forest. In the valley beyond stands Pluscarden Abbey, rebuilt by the community of Benedictine monks who moved there in 1948, after the site had been out of their Order's hands since the Reformation. Visitors are welcome.

North-west of Elgin, the ruins of the 13th-century Duffus Castle, to a Norman motte-and-bailey design, are open to view. A mile farther north is Gordonstoun School, of which several members of the Royal Family are old boys.

On the coast, the five miles of

Although Elgin Cathedral was badly damaged many times, much of its early 13th-century work remains preserved

sandy beaches on Burghead Bay can be reached either from the fishing village of Burghead itself, or from the Forestry Commission's picnic site among the pinewoods of Roseisle on the B9089.

AA recommends:

Garage: Sher Morr (A D Scott), Sheriffmill, *tel.* 7121 (day), Lhanbryde 3091 (night)

Floating Timber

Vast areas of the old Caledonian Pine Forest were felled in the 18th and 19th centuries. Getting the timber to sawmills, seaports and boat-building yards, in the days before good roads and any railways, could be done only by river.

Beside some of the burns in the Black Wood of Rannoch, for instance, there were wooden flumes, down which, when the water was diverted into them, logs would hurtle to the lochside below. The remains of dams which held back logs cut in the forests of Abernethy and Rothiemurchus can still be seen at the west end of Loch Morlich and Loch an Eilein, and on the River Nethy above Nethy Bridge. On the other side of the Cairngorms, there was another dam in Glen Derry, above Derry Lodge.

Once the timber was gathered in the main river, the floaters took over. Their job was to build the logs into rafts, which they steered down-river to the sea.

On the Spey, the destinations were the timber and boat-yards of Garmouth and Kingston. On the Dee, rafts of pine and oak from the forests of Glentanar were assembled at Aboyne, then piloted to the docks at Aberdeen.

River Findhorn

Map Ref: 88NH8232

From its source in the lonely deer forests of the Monadliath Hills, the Findhorn winds down Strathdearn to Tomatin on the A9, and is then lost to the motorist's view as it proceeds by the harshly eroded valley of the Streens, to reappear beside a public road at Drynachan Lodge. Below Drynachan is Dulsie Bridge, built by military road-gangs in the 1750s over a spectacular rocky gorge.

A few miles downstream is the all but hidden 17th-century church of Ardclach. It was so low-set that the parishioners could not always hear the church bell. So a separate bell-tower, which can be visited, was set on the hillside above.

Near the northern end of the B9007, the Findhorn's splendidly wooded course takes it splashing through the rock pools at Randolph's Leap, scene of an agile fugitive's 14th-century escape.

Then the river meanders past the town of Forres before flowing into Findhorn Bay, with the sailing resort of Findhorn on the east bank and the extensive plantations of Culbin Forest, once a wilderness of sand dunes, on the west.

AA recommends:
Garage: Falcon Motors, Greshop Industrial Estate, Forres, *tel.* 74709

Salmon-fishing in the River Tay

Salmon rivers

The best salmon rivers in the Highlands can be fished in a remarkable variety of locations. Some anglers favour the riverbanks well within the town boundaries of Perth and Inverness. Others wade chest-deep at Grantown in the darkening waters of a Speyside dusk. There are famous salmon beats in the remote headwaters of northern rivers such as the Oykel and the Halladale; along the wooded banks of the Findhorn and the Deveron; on the Dee and the Don before they meet the North Sea at Aberdeen.

Pride of place among the salmon rivers goes to the Tay. Together with its many tributaries, like the Tummel and the Lyon, it has the greatest catchment area of any river in Britain. More than 10,000 salmon are caught in these waters every season — and that is without counting the many times more netted at commercial stations on the Firth.

The Tay still holds the record for the heaviest salmon ever caught on a British river. Husky anglers have been trying for 60 years to match the 67½ lb fish taken on the Glendelvine beat downriver from Birnam — after a four-hour struggle — by a no doubt tired, but triumphant, 22-year-old girl, Georgina Ballantine.

Top and right: some of the antiquities and a tableau which form part of Fort William's West Highland Museum Above: Ardlach church, so low-lying that it needed a separate bell-tower

Fort William

Map Ref: 91NN1074

Situated on the shore of the right-angled Loch Eil, at the southern end of the Great Glen which strikes directly through Scotland from Inverness, Fort William is the trading and transport centre of Lochaber, spreading up the foothills of Ben Nevis, the highest mountain in Britain.

A government fortress of 1655 was rebuilt much more strongly during the reign of William III and gave the town its name. But the fort was swept away in 1864 to make room for the railway, whose arrival sparked off the building of the modern town. Fort William is one of the principal stations on the West Highland Line from Glasgow. Trains continue beyond it through rugged scenery by Glenfinnan and a famous viaduct, Lochailort, Arisaig and Morar to the herring port of Mallaig and a car-ferry to Skye.

Fort William's West Highland museum includes many relics of Jacobite times, notably the 'secret portrait' of Prince Charles Edward Stuart – Bonnie Prince Charlie. A wooden board has an apparently random design of daubs of paint. But when a metal cylinder is placed on it, the multi-coloured streaks reflect on its curved surface as a miniature portrait of the Prince.

There are two famous sporting events in Fort William, both testing competitors' stamina to its limits. In May, the town is the base for the Scottish Six Days' Trial, an endurance motor-cycling event which attracts top riders from all over the world. September is the time of the Ben Nevis Race, when runners tackle a course from the Claggan Park to the summit of the 4406ft mountain and back again.

Ben Nevis shows its least spectacular side to the town. From Achintee, at the end of the road along the east side of Glen Nevis, the 'tourist path' climbs wearisomely to the summit.

However, although the summit can sometimes be shrouded in cloud even when the sun is shining in Fort William, the view from the top on a clear day is magnificent. Southwards are the mountain ridges of the lonely Mamores, west is Ardgour. Much farther away, the view extends to the Cairngorms and the island peaks of Jura and Skye.

On the north side of Ben Nevis are the mighty 2000ft rock faces, towers, gullies and buttresses which attract mountaineers, summer and winter. On the plateau itself are the ruins of the observatory established in 1883 by the meteorologist Clement Wragge. This did pioneering work in long-range weather forecasting, before being thoughtlessly closed down in 1904.

For people who prefer lower altitudes, the great spectacle in Glen Nevis is the mile-long echoing gorge among the pines and birches below Steall. It is reached by footpath from the car park at the top of the main Glen Nevis road.

Lower down the glen there are walks in the Forestry Commission plantations which form almost the final stretch of the West Highland

Way. More forest walks have been laid out at Leanachan on the Spean Bridge road and at Inchree uphill from Corran Ferry, south of Fort William. This car-ferry is the main link to Ardgour and Ardnamurchan. By the lochside, off the A82, there are some very pleasant picnic sites.

North of Fort William, a left turn off the A82 leads on to the A830, the Road to the Isles towards Mallaig. The A830 goes via Banavie, where the Caledonian Canal starts with the eight locks of Thomas Telford's Neptune's Staircase, the longest flight of canal locks in Scotland.

Perhaps the strangest sight in the mountain country around Fort William is in Glen Roy, north-east of Spean Bridge, from a Nature Conservancy car park and viewpoint. On the lonely hillsides to the north are the 'Parallel Roads', stretching for miles in a horseshoe curve round the glen.

They mark the three different shore levels of an ice age loch, progressively lower as the ice which dammed it melted, until finally water and ice both completely drained away. The whole of the upper glen is a nature reserve with an unspoiled range of hill country, and gives a unique insight into Scotland's glacial past.

AA recommends:

Hotel: Inverlochy Castle (3m NE A82), 2-rosette, 4-red star, *tel.* 2177

Self Catering: Glen Nevis Holiday Cottages, Glen Nevis, *tel.* 2191
Great Glen Holidays, *tel.* 3015
Innseagan Apartments, Achintore Road, *tel.* 2452

Guesthouses: Benview, Belford Road, *tel.* 2966
Guisachan, Alma Road, *tel.* 3797
Hillview, Achintore Road, *tel.* 4349
Innseagan, Achintore Road, *tel.* 2452
Lochview, Heathcroft, Argyll Road, *tel.* 3149
Rhu Mhor, Alma Road, *tel.* 2213
Stronchreggan View, Achintore Road, *tel.* 4644

Garage: Ben Car Sales, Ardgour Road, Caol, *tel.* 2408 (day), Corpach 461 (night)

Glenfinnan's superb mountain setting for the Jacobite monument, erected in 1815 at the head of Loch Shiel

Gairloch

Map Ref: 86NG8076

Spread along the shore of a west-facing sea-loch, Gairloch is a self-contained holiday resort in beautifully varied coastal, hill and mountain scenery. It has splendid sands, a golf course where even novices ('rabbits') are consoled by the views, sea angling in Loch Gairloch, fishing in rivers and inland lochs, and it is the centre for attractive drives in every direction.

Gairloch village and its satellite settlements like Strath and Auchtercairn are built along the A832 and the B8021 which runs along the north shore of Loch Gairloch. At Auchtercairn, the Gairloch Heritage Museum is open on weekdays from May till September. The harbour, tucked away in a sheltered bay to the south, is the base of Gairloch Boat Club.

The most intriguing stretch of Loch Gairloch is its southern shore, a series of wooded and rocky inlets. It is reached by the B8056, meandering towards Badachro, where boats may be hired and the bay is completely sheltered by the bulk of Eilean Horrisdale.

Then the countryside changes. Trees are few and far between. Settlements like Port Henderson and Opinan, with its curving beach and windswept sand drifting over the road, look out on the open sea. At Redpoint, not long before the road ends, there are more sandy bays, grassy dunes and a viewpoint looking west towards Skye, south and east towards the shapely peaks of Torridon.

North-west from Gairloch, the B8021 goes past the camping and caravan sites at Little Sand on the way up the coast to Melvaig, where it

View from Gairloch towards the distant Torridon mountains of Wester Ross

A smoke tree in Inverewe Gardens

becomes the private road to the lighthouse at Rubha Reidh.

North-eastwards, the A832 heads briefly inland by Loch Tollie and the side-road to Tollie Bay on Loch Maree, to the village of Poolewe. It lies at the head of Loch Ewe, an anchorage for convoys during the second world war and still with naval connections today.

The B8057 turns off to follow the west side of the loch, through the crofting townships around Inverasdale. It finishes at a rough track, better tackled on foot, to a hilltop viewpoint.

North of Poolewe the main road passes the National Trust for Scotland's garden at Inverewe. Open daily throughout the year, it was created from a wilderness of rock and heather by Osgood Mackenzie, who started the project in 1862.

Beyond Inverewe, a private garden occasionally open to the public is at Tournaig. There are fine high-level viewpoints on the winding stretch from there to Aultbea, where a side-road to the left leads to the surprisingly extensive crofting settlement of Mellon Charles.

The A832 heads over the hills again to come down to sea level at Laide, a village with a sandy beach on Gruinard Bay. A pleasant side-road towards Mellon Udrigle turns left at Laide, and another smaller road off it, signposted to Laide Jetty, leads to a picnic site by a rock and shingle shore.

Farther along the Mellon Udrigle road, a tarred then rough-surfaced track goes left over heather moor and peat moss, past quiet lochans which can, with permission, be fished for

trout, to the remote and ruined crofting township of Slaggan. A footpath leads to a lonely sandy beach, where Atlantic breakers come rolling in.

Continuing north beyond the Slaggan turn-off, the Mellon Udrigle road passes close to Loch na Beiste – the Loch of the Beast – where a 19th-century estate owner unavailingly pursued a monster which some of his tenants insisted they had seen. Mellon Udrigle itself is one of the most beautiful places on the coast. A wide sandy bay (with plenty of parking space) looks north-east across Loch Broom to the mountain peaks of Coigach.

One more side-turning to the left at Mellon Udrigle leads to the scattered houses of Opinan, which is really the end of the road, with still more sandy beaches and a coastline deeply indented with rocky inlets. One of the houses at Opinan is also an art gallery.

AA recommends:
Self Catering: Gairloch Sands Apartments, *tel.* 2131
Millcroft Hotel, *tel.* 2376
Guesthouse: Horisdale House, Strath, *tel.* 2151

Glamis

Map Ref: 93NO3846

The two main visitor attractions in this pleasant little Angus village could hardly be more different in size and style. In the village itself, the National Trust for Scotland maintains the Kirkwynd Cottages – a row of 17th-century almshouses – as the Angus Folk Museum.

The Kirkwynd is also well-known for its Jacquard loom. Most of these elsewhere are simply display pieces, but the Glamis example is used by the only handloom linen weaver working regularly in Scotland at a craft which used to support entire villages.

North of the village, in wooded parkland bounded by the Dean Water, Glamis Castle is the home of the Bowes-Lyon Earls of Strathmore. The present castle is a massive, ornamentally-towered building of the 17th century, with beautifully furnished state rooms open to visitors.

Elizabeth Bowes-Lyon (the Queen Mother) married the Duke of York, who later became George VI; and Princess Margaret was born at Glamis in 1930.

AA recommends:
Self Catering: The Croft, Tomich, nr Cannich, *tel.* Cannich 220
Guesthouse: Dunire, Glencoe, *tel.* Ballachulish 318
Scorrybreac, Glencoe, *tel.* Ballachulish 354

Top right: rustic Kirkwynd Cottages at Glamis form the Angus Folk Museum

National Trust for Scotland wall plaque

Below: 14th-century Glamis castle was later rebuilt in French-château style

Start of the Glen Clova hill tracks

Glen Affric

Map Ref: 87NH2020

Although it has one of the most beautiful landscapes in Scotland, with slender lochs in the valley floor, well-wooded hillsides and a river rising among the 3000ft mountains at its head, Glen Affric has been greatly altered by two separate interests.

In 1946 the North of Scotland and Hydro-Electric Board dammed the River Affric to create the five-mile Loch Benevean. Its power station at Fasnakyle is unobtrusively located and faced with local yellow sandstone. The two waterfalls in the narrow Affric gorge – the Badger Fall and the Dog Fall – remain as they always were.

Both sides of the glen are cloaked in Forestry Commission plantations. A determined effort is being made to help Glen Affric's remnant of the old Caledonian Pine Forest extend and regenerate. Forest walks and picnic places have been laid out beside the Dog Fall.

Glen Clova

Map Ref: 92NO3273

This is the grandest of the Angus glens, draining the headwaters of the River South Esk. The circular-route B955 goes as far as Milton of Clova, from which a dead-end road continues to a picnic site in the Glendoll section of Braes of Angus Forest. Glendoll youth hostel, a former shooting lodge, is 1000ft above sea level.

Two famous hill tracks head over the high passes towards Deeside. The Tolmounth reaches more than 2800ft on the way to Braemar. The Capel Mounth rises to 2250ft as it makes for Loch Muick and Ballater. Shorter trails in the spruce and larch plantations give a taste of the clean air, the untamed mountain scenery and the sense of freedom which take climbers back to Glen Clova time and time again.

Dog Fall – unchanged despite events

Glencoe

With its mixture of overwhelming mountain scenery and a tragic history, which includes a massacre of clansmen still bitterly remembered today, no easily-reached glen in Scotland is as atmospheric as Glencoe, especially when cloud and mist are wreathed round its towering peaks and ridges. Certainly no trunk road in Britain seems quite as insignificant as the A82 as it threads its way along the foot of the glen.

From the south-east, the A82 reaches Glencoe over a summit above the Rannoch Moor, then makes a long gradual descent. It passes a side-road to the left towards the chairlift up to the Glencoe skiing grounds, and the loop road on the right to Kingshouse Hotel, originally a staging post on the 18th-century military road to Fort William.

Another side-road on the left down Glen Etive, before the beautifully proportioned peak of Buachaille Etive Mor — the Great Shepherd of Etive — marks the boundary of the National Trust for Scotland's Glencoe estate. More than 14,000 acres in the glen, including the best rock-climbing areas, are in the Trust's hands, yet access to them is unrestricted.

This is the start of the 'real' Glencoe, and although the mountains themselves are for rock-climbers, several more straightforward walking routes cut through them. Set among a patch of woodland to the right of the main road, the house of Altnafeadh marks the start of the Devil's Staircase over the northern ridge to Kinlochleven. This hairpinned route was part of the military road. Now it is included in the West Highland Way and — more incongruously — is used every year by motorcyclists competing in the Scottish Six Days' Trial.

Opposite Altnafeadh, a footbridge over the River Coe leads to one of several walking tracks into the steep-sided glens on the south side. All these routes are, of course, for properly-equipped and experienced hill-walkers.

Beyond Loch Achtriochtan in the valley floor, the main road swings right, out of the most precipitous part of Glencoe, to the National Trust for Scotland's visitor centre, open daily from April to October. Here there is a description of the events of the massacre of February 1692, when a party of troops billetted on the MacDonalds of Glencoe rose in the night and, acting on secret orders, tried to murder all their hosts — the clan chief and his wife, men, women and children.

A footpath from the visitor centre, over a bridge across the Coe, leads through woodlands to Signal Rock, where, according to tradition, the signal to start the attack was given. Another walk from the same place goes to a fine viewpoint at An Torr, looking eastwards into the mountainous heart of the glen and north to the great gully above Clachaig Inn. That gully is one of the boundaries of the 'cauldron subsidence' caused in prehistoric times, when the centre of the volcano which occupied most of modern Glencoe collapsed, and a huge outpouring of molten granite surged up in its place.

The village of Glencoe is on much lower ground, near the shore of Loch Leven. It lies along both sides of the old Glencoe road, superseded by the present one in the 1930s. Halfway towards another bridge over the Coe is the Glencoe and North Lorn Folk Museum, open on weekdays from May to September. Close by is St Mary's church, with its memorial to the last of the MacDonald chiefs of Glencoe, who died in 1894. A side-road to the right, immediately before the bridge, leads to the monument to the MacDonalds killed in 1692.

The village is dominated by the splendidly regular conical peak of Sgor na Ciche, the 2430ft Pap of Glencoe. Beyond the bridge, a turning to the left leads to the Lochan Trail, laid out by the Forestry Commission in the woodlands on its lower slopes.

Centrepiece of the trail is the walk round the lochan itself, with rhododendrons in profusion along the edges and a bordering hillside of tall Corsican pines. One sight no visitor to Glencoe should miss is the reflection of the Pap of Glencoe, and other mountains as the circular walk progresses, mirrored on a calm day in the clear waters of this most attractive ornamental lake.

Glenelg

Map Ref: 86NG8119

One of the most exhilarating drives in Scotland is over the narrow, hairpinned pass of Mam Ratagan to Glenelg on the Sound of Sleat. A right turn at Glenelg leads past pleasant picknicking areas to the summer-only car ferry to Kylerhea on Skye. The left turn through the main part of the village passes the substantial ruins of the Hanoverian barracks built after 1719 to keep the Jacobite Highlanders in check.

South of Glenelg, up a side-road along the wooded valley of the Glenbeag River, are the brochs of Dun Telve and Dun Troddan, tall beehive-shaped stone houses occupied 2000 years ago by families of Picts.

The coast road sweeps over the shoulder of the mountains above Loch Hourn. A forest track leads down to Sandaig, the site of 'Camusfearna' in Gavin Maxwell's *Ring of Bright Water*.

Once out of the forest, the road plunges down to Arnisdale and Corran, beautifully situated villages on the north shore of Loch Hourn. Across the loch are the 3000ft-high peaks of Knoydart. The road ends at Corran, a cluster of houses, where in spring the gardens are a blaze of daffodils.

Glen Esk

Map Ref: 89NO4979

Compared with Glen Clova, Glen Esk has a much gentler landscape, although a footpath from Gannachy Bridge on the B956 goes alongside the ravine where the River North Esk tumbles through the tangled rocks of the Highland Boundary Fault.

There is a pleasant stroll from Invermark near the head of the glen,

Part of lovely Dunrobin Glen, Golspie

which leads to a most majestic extravagance, in the shape of a 20ft-high stone replica of the Imperial Crown. Queen Victoria came this way in 1861 and the monument was built over the Queen's Well, where she paused while taking a pony ride.

At Tarfside, mementoes of farming and domestic life, fiddles and firearms, mining and whisky-smuggling, are gathered in the Glenesk Folk Museum, open on Sundays from Easter, then daily from June to September.

Glen Lyon

Map Ref: 91NN5245

From the high-level reservoir of Loch Lyon in the remote mountains of Mamlorn – part of the massive, but generally unobtrusive, Breadalbane hydro-electric scheme – the River Lyon winds down a narrow valley to the comfortable village of Fortingall. Its course of more than 30 miles is through the longest glen in Scotland. An attractive road follows the often wooded riverside between towering hills given over mostly to sheep and deer.

Fortingall village owes its thatched houses to a late-Victorian landlord. In the churchyard, the Fortingall yew is one of the oldest living things in Europe, planted at least 1500 years ago. Even further back into the mists of history, if a local tradition is true, this is where Pontius Pilate was born, while his father guarded the hills and glens with a Roman legion.

AA recommends:
Self Catering: Aberfeldy Country Cottages, Moness Farm, Aberfeldy, *tel.* 20851
Guesthouses: Balnearn Private Hotel, Crieff Road, Aberfeldy, *tel.* 20431
Caber Feidh, 66 Dunkeld Street, Aberfeldy, *tel.* 20342
Guinach House, Urlar Road, Aberfeldy, *tel.* 20251
Nessbank House, Crieff Road, Aberfeldy, *tel.* 20214
Tom of Cluny (Farmhouse), Aberfeldy, *tel.* 20477

Hydro-electric Power

Although the first privately-operated hydro-electric power stations in Scotland were built in the 1890s, large-scale development of this natural resource was delayed until the establishment, in 1943, of the North of Scotland Hydro-Electric Board. The Board provides power over a quarter of the total land-mass of Britain.

Many of its later developments harmonise remarkably well with their surroundings. Power stations are often faced with authentic local stone. At Pitlochry, the Board's headquarters, the creation of the winding and wooded Loch Faskally has added one more attraction to an already beautiful scene.

Pitlochry is also the site of the best-known of the Board's fish-passes, built to allow salmon unrestricted access, beyond the dam, to their spawning grounds upstream. Through glass panels, visitors can watch the salmon battling their way against the flow, just as they do in a natural river.

The most spectacular place open to the public in the Board's extensive domain is the power station literally *under* Ben Cruachan in Argyll. Visitors are taken in a minibus, along an access road through a tunnel two-thirds of a mile long, to the generating hall, 120ft high, in the very heart of the mountain.

Huntly

Map Ref: 89NJ5339

Once the stronghold of the Gordons – and Gordon is still the district name today – Huntly was extended according to a street plan drawn up by the Duke of Gordon in 1776. Two architecture trails start from Huntly Museum in the town square.

Castle Street leads to an avenue past the Gordon Schools – founded, inevitably, by a Duchess of Gordon in 1839 – to Huntly Castle. The first castle, on a mound above the banks of the River Deveron, was in Norman style. The present ruins are of a much grander castle built at the start of the 17th century by a Marquess of Huntly impressed by the Renaissance architecture of a château on the Loire.

Southwards off the B9002 near Kennethmont, is Leith Hall, a 17th-century house and 236-acre hillside estate owned by the National Trust for Scotland. The house is open from May to September; the gardens and nature trails are open all year.

Inveraray

Map Ref: 91NN0908

In the 1740s, the 3rd Duke of Argyll began the 50-year task of building Inveraray Castle in its wooded parkland above Loch Fyne. Unfortunately, the old burgh of Inveraray stood in the way, so he had it demolished and a new town, in the best spirit of Georgian architecture and planning, established nearby.

A full-scale restoration project that began back in 1957, has seen most of the Georgian public and domestic buildings completely renovated. Their white-washed walls reflect in the waters of a tidal bay.

Inveraray Castle itself – still the home of the Dukes of Argyll, chiefs of Clan Campbell – is open to the public from April to October, although closed on Fridays except in July and August. At Cherry Park in the grounds, a Combined Operations Museum recalls Inverary's role as a second world war Commando training base.

An excellent walk to a magnificent hilltop viewpoint starts in the castle grounds, while in the town, there is a lower-level viewpoint at a bell-tower built in the 1920s with a famous peal of bells installed as a Campbell war memorial.

South of Inveraray, the Loch Fyneside road passes the Argyll Wildfowl Park at Dalchenna, the farming museum at the old township of Auchindrain, and the spectacular woodland gardens in Crarae Glen.

AA recommends:
Garages: Dalmally Road Garage, Dalmally Road, *tel.* 2473
Shore Street (W D Semple), *tel.* 2150

Golspie

Map Ref: 85NH8399

A self-contained place, and the administrative centre of Sutherland, Golspie grew up after the early 19th-century clearances on the inland parts of the 1st Duke of Sutherland's estates. But St Andrew's church was built in 1619, although its canopied pulpit and 'laird's loft' are from a century later.

Behind a long sandy beach there is a fine links golf course. On the road to Littleferry and the tidal flats of the Loch Fleet nature reserve, a kart-racing track which attracts competitors from all over Scotland is hidden in the dunes.

There are enjoyable climbing

One of the Glenelg brochs, whose thick walls protected Picts against invaders

walks in the pinewoods behind the town, and along the paths and rustic bridges in Dunrobin Glen. Dunrobin Castle, seat of the present Duke of Sutherland, was extended in the 19th century and has gardens modelled on those at Versailles.

AA recommends:
Self Catering: Log Cabin, Backies, *tel.* Stamford 63365 (weekends & evenings) & 52075 (office hours)
Guesthouses: Glenshee, Station Road, *tel.* 3254
Park House Hotel (Inn), Main Street, *tel.* 3667
Garages: Golspie Motors, Station Road, *tel.* 3205

Inverness

Map Ref: 88NH6645

Inverness, the capital of the Highlands, spreads along the banks of the River Ness. Near the Victorian Town House, an excellent local museum and art gallery is open on weekdays throughout the year. On the hilltop above the museum, Inverness Castle is an imposing building of delicate red sandstone, built between 1834 and 1847 as a Sheriff Court and jail.

There is a pleasant walk along the riverside, over footbridges on to the wooded Ness Islands. A steeper forest trail, west of the town, goes to the summit of Craig Phadrig, possibly the location of the fortress-capital of the Pictish kings.

Culloden Moor, site of the last pitched battle on British soil, which ended the Jacobite Rising in 1746, is eastwards on the B9006. A National Trust for Scotland visitor centre there is open from April to October.

North-east of Inverness, the mid 18th-century Fort George is

The famous Soldier's Leap in the Pass of Killiecrankie

on a heavily-defended peninsula into the Moray Firth. Although Fort George is still a military establishment, part of it is open as an Ancient Monument, and it also houses the regimental museums of the Seaforth and the Cameron Highlanders.

Across the new Kessock Bridge, on the Black Isle, there are forest walks above North Kessock. Fortrose and Rosemarkie are sailing and golfing resorts. Fulmars nest on the cliffs beyond Rosemarkie, while pinkfoot and greylag geese roost on the tidal inlet of Munlochy Bay.

AA recommends:
Hotels: Culloden House, Culloden Moor (2m E off A96), 4-star, Country House Hotel, *tel.* 790461
Dunain Park, 1-rosette, 2-red star, Country House Hotel, *tel.* 230512
Self Catering: Fuinary Cottage, 10A Culduthel Road, *tel.* Dochgarroch 247
Guesthouses: For a selection of guesthouses, please consult the AA guide *Guesthouses, Farmhouses and Inns in Britain.*
Garage: Cordiners, Harbour Road, *tel.* 238001 (day), 236380 (night)

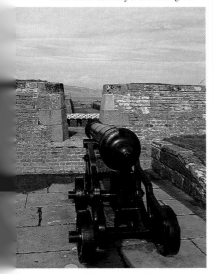

Cannon at Fort George near Inverness

Inverness Castle, built of pink sandstone, was once a court and jail

Inverurie

Map Ref: 89NJ7721

Built where the River Urie, meandering desperately over an all but level valley floor, finally manages to merge with the Don, this is a substantial town in its own right, as well as the main shopping and business centre for the district of Garioch – known as 'the Geerie'.

Inverurie is ringed by a great number of prehistoric sites, from 4000 year-old circles of standing stones to Pictish carvings. Some of these are to be found in the cemetery, which was an important location in later Pictish times: the grassy hill within the cemetery bounds was the site of a long-disappeared Norman castle.

Nearby, across the Don, the suburb of Port Elphinstone justifies its name because it was the start of a 19th-century canal to Aberdeen. There is a display of canal relics in the fine museum in Inverurie's market place.

AA recommends:
Hotel: Gordon Arms, The Square, 1-star, *tel.* 20314

Killiecrankie

Map Ref: 92NN9162

A battlefield, a village and a chasm through which the River Garry tumbles between steeply-wooded cliffs, all take the same name here. The Battle of Killiecrankie in 1689 was a success for the Jacobites.

It is a member of General

Sunset across Loch Hourn, a remote classic fiord surrounded by mountains

Mackay's defeated army, fighting for William III, who is remembered at the Soldier's Leap in the Pass of Killiecrankie. He hurled himself across the gorge, and his pursuer – wisely – declined to follow.

A National Trust for Scotland visitor centre is open daily from April to October. And the Trust has laid out two nature trails at the Linn of Tummel, through the beautiful and varied woodlands where the Tummel and the Garry meet.

AA recommends:
Hotel: Killiecrankie, I-rosette, 2-star, *tel.* Pitlochry 3220
Self Catering: Old Faskally Chalets, *tel.* Pitlochry 3436
Guesthouse: Dalnasgadh House, *tel.* Pitlochry 3237

Kinlochhourn

Map Ref: 87NG9506

One of the remotest places reached by public road in mainland Britain, at the head of Loch Hourn, a classic fiord. The only patch of level ground is around a farm and a shooting lodge. Everywhere else, the mountains rear up from the water's edge; there are wild rocky outcrops to the south, but less rumpled, birchwood-covered slopes on the north side.

A rough footpath heads along the south shore. Behind the lodge, another path goes north-west towards Arnisdale.

The lonely road to Kinlochhourn, overlooked by the jagged peaks of Knoydart, becomes narrower and steeper in its final plunge to the sea-loch. Outside the stalking season, drivers may be delayed by red deer browsing at the roadside.

AA recommends:
Guesthouse: No. 3 Greenfield, Tomdown (farmhouse), *tel.* Tomdown 221

Deer Forests

Deer forests from Deeside up to distant Lochnagar over Balmoral Forest

There are four species of wild deer in the Highlands. Fallow deer and Japanese Sika deer were originally established in deer parks, like the fallow deer on the Loch Lomond island of Inchlonaig. Roe deer are much more widespread, in woodlands and on the hills.

The *Monarch of the Glen*, however, the subject of Sir Edwin Landseer's famous Victorian painting, is undoubtedly the red deer, Scotland's biggest native wild animal. Something like 200,000 live in the Highlands and Islands.

In many areas, red-deer stalking is an important part of the local economy. High rentals are paid for good stalking grounds, and venison is exported. Stalking takes place among the lonely crags and corries of the deer forests — but these are forests almost entirely without trees.

Red deer stags may be shot from July 1 to October 20, and during that season hill-walkers and climbers should always check whether they are likely to disturb a carefully-organised stalk.

In summer, red deer are usually high in the hills, feeding on the new season's grass. But they will sometimes be seen late at night, dramatically caught in the beam of a car's headlights, as they cross a road on the way to drink from the river in a glen.

Kintail

Map Ref: 87NG9319

The Five Sisters of Kintail are among the most shapely mountain peaks in Scotland. As the A87 road comes down to the sea at Loch Duich, through Glen Shiel, the south-western boundary of the range, it passes the site of the battle of 1719. It was here that Spanish troops, supporting the abortive Jacobite Rising, were put to flight.

Like other hill ground in Kintail, the Five Sisters are owned by the National Trust for Scotland, which has an information centre at Morvich, on a bypassed stretch of the old main road.

Loch Duich is forested on both sides. The narrow minor road, from Shiel Bridge below the hill plantations of Ratagan Forest to Totaig, continues as a footpath to an exhilarating viewpoint over sea-lochs and mountains.

Across Loch Duich at Dornie on the A87, a causeway leads to the island fortress of Eilean Donan which was reduced to rubble by a naval bombardment during the 1719 Rising. Completely restored in the 1930s, the castle is open daily from April to October.

Lochalsh woodland

Kyle of Lochalsh

Map Ref: 86NG7627

Beyond Dornie the A87 enters the district of Lochalsh, much of which is included in the National Trust for Scotland's Balmacara estate. Balmacara village has a picnic site by the shore of Loch Alsh, and a fine variety of hill and woodland walks. Down a side-road there are meandering pathways through the Trust's Lochalsh Woodland Garden, which is open all year. A visitor centre is open from April to October.

After Balmacara, the A87 reaches Kyle of Lochalsh, the car-ferry port for the short crossing to Skye and also, in summer, for the northern end of a passenger steamer service through the Sound of Sleat from Mallaig.

Kyle is the shopping, trading and transport centre of the district. A short walk to the summit of the Ploc of Kyle shows off the coastline of rugged, rocky bays; reefs and offshore islands; and – across the narrow strait – the hill and mountain country of Skye.

North-east of Kyle, on a winding inlet of Loch Carron, Plockton is one of the most beautifully situated villages in Scotland, with palm-trees growing in lochside gardens and mountains all around. This is an excellent centre for walking and sailing, and has its own popular summer regatta.

Left: shapely Five Sisters of Kintail above Loch Duich

Golden autumn at Eilean Donan Castle, Loch Duich

Highland Clearances

Many places in the Highlands have not always been as deserted as they are today. Long-ruined cottages and the encroachment of rushes where once-cultivated land has gone back to the wild are clear evidence of that.

There were several causes of Highland depopulation in the 18th and 19th centuries — too many people for the land; a potato famine; the appeal of making a better life overseas.

But many great landowners and their agents decided to make more money from their estates, through renting the land for sheep-farming and, later, for deer-stalking, than could be raised from subsistence-level smallholders.

Many of the evictions, notably in Sutherland and in Knoydart, were brutal. Men, women and children, the elderly, the sick and the infirm were thrown out of their homes, which were then demolished. They had no option but to emigrate, move to the cities or to one of the settlements newly established on the coast.

Smallholders had no legal protection until the first Crofters Act of 1886. By then, many of the glens were already deserted. 'Clearances' is all too bland a word for the deliberate policy of emptying a countryside to make way for sheep and deer.

Lairg

Map Ref: 84NC5806

The most important road centre in the heart of Sutherland, with a station on the Inverness-Wick railway, Lairg has been settled for a very long time. The moorlands all around are dotted with the sites of prehistoric cairns and stone age dwellings.

Nowadays, Lairg is best known for its livestock sales and for being a place which provides fine trout and salmon fishing. It is at the edge of Loch Shin, which has fish-passes at its hydro-electric dam to allow salmon free passage upstream. South of the loch, the River Shin passes through a narrow, wooded valley. There is a famous salmon leap at the Falls of Shin, reached by a Forestry Commission trail.

AA recommends:
Self Catering: The Hotel Apartment, *tel.* 2291
The Cottage, *tel.* 2291
Garden Cottages, *tel.* 2291
Guesthouses: Carnbren, *tel.* 2259
Alt-Na-Sorag (farmhouse), 14 Achnairn, *tel.* 2058
5 Terryside (farmhouse), *tel.* 2332
Garage: Sutherland Transport & Trading Company, Main Street, *tel.* 2465

Top: *winter colours on the hills above Kilchurn Castle, Loch Awe*

Above: *St Conan's Kirk, Loch Awe*

Left: *The Falls of Shin*

Iron-working

Scotland's earliest ironworks were in the Highlands, where huge tracts of natural woodland were felled to provide charcoal for the furnaces in which imported ore was smelted. As early as 1607 the native oakwoods of Loch Maree were being plundered. Now, only the place-name Furnace on the north-eastern shore remains as an incongruous reminder, among the mountains, of a long-gone trade.

Of the many charcoal ironworks — or 'bloomeries' — in the Highlands, the best known is the Lorn Furnace at Bonawe on the southern shore of Loch Etive. Richard Ford and Company of Furness in Lancashire, using ore shipped in from Ulverston, produced its first iron here in 1753.

The Lorn Furnace, by then hopelessly out of date, went out of business in the 1870s. Rescued from dereliction and carefuly restored, it is now open as an Ancient Monument. Part of the woodland which provided its charcoal is preserved too, in the twin National Nature Reserve and Forest Nature Reserve in Glen Nant, to the south. The old charcoal-burners' tracks can still be walked on a nature trail, and the coppiced oakwoods show that, here at least, the ironmasters worked with some sense of the need to conserve supplies.

Loch Awe

Map Ref: 90NM9710

The north shore of Loch Awe is reached by the A85 Dalmally-Oban road, which squeezes between the lochside and the great bulk of Ben Cruachan at the steep-sided Pass of Brander. On the lochside there, the North of Scotland Hydro-Electric Board's visitor centre is open from April to October and offers a chance to see underground workings of the Cruachan scheme.

Lochawe village has several hotels which offer trout and salmon fishing. St Conan's Kirk, completed in 1930, includes a deliberate but bewildering variety of architectural styles.

The east side of Loch Awe is reached by the beautifully wooded A819, with views to the ruined Campbell stronghold of Kilchurn Castle, and then the winding B840 by Portinnisherrich and the fringe of Eredine Forest to Ford. From there, a narrow road with blind summits heads back up the west side through the plantations of Inverliever and Inverinan. The Forestry Commission has several walks and trails here, with splendid views and varied wildlife.

At Kilchrenan, a dead-end road leads to gardens of conifers, maples and flowering shrubs. The gardens are open from April to October. Back-tracking to Kilchrenan, the last link in the circuit of Loch Awe is the road through Glen Nant and its forest reserves, which rejoins the A85 near Taynuilt.

AA recommends:
Hotel: Carraig-Thura Lochawe, 2-star, *tel.* Dalmally 210

Loch Earn

Map Ref: 91NN6223

Lochearnhead is the home of water-skiing in Scotland, and the loch is also popular with dinghy sailors, canoeists and trout fishermen. The A85 runs past wooded bays and picnic places on the north shore to St Fillans, where the Forestry Commission's Glentarken walk wanders through old oakwoods above the village.

On the other side of the loch, a narrower road goes along the foot of the southern hills which soar up to the 3224ft summit of Ben Vorlich. The gardens of Ardvorlich House, with many species of rhododendron growing in a glen, are occasionally open to the public. A hill-walker's track goes up Glen Ample, overlooked by the crags on the western outliers of Ben Vorlich, to cross a pass and then descend steeply through the forest plantations to Loch Lubnaig.

AA recommends:
Hotels: Lochearnhead, Lochside, 1-star, *tel.* Lochearnhead 229
Mansewood Country House, Lochearnhead, 1-star, *tel.* 213
Self Catering: Lochearn Lodges, Lochearnhead, *tel.* 211

Watersport centre at Lochearnhead

Crofting

Although many Highland estates cover tens of thousands of acres, something like two million acres in the Highlands and Islands, Orkney and Shetland, are occupied by crofts. Each of these individual smallholdings may consist of several different parts. There will be arable ground near the house, most likely a share in hill grazings for sheep and cattle, and, in suitable areas, a share in a peat moss, which will — after a few weeks of very hard work — provide fuel for a whole year at no cost in cash.

Use of the common grazings around crofting villages, usually called townships, is arranged by an elected grazings committee. And much of the work at busy times is shared among neighbours. The general regulation of crofting, including transfers of land, loans and grants for improvements, is done by the Crofters Commission in Inverness.

Many crofters have full-time or part-time jobs elsewhere, perhaps in fishing or forestry, or work the crofts in retirement. Occasionally, a crofter will have amalgamated several smaller holdings into something nearer in size to a conventional farm.

A hospitable croft will provide ideal holiday accommodation, especially in districts off the beaten track.

Rough and tough, but a croft may not be everybody's desirable residence

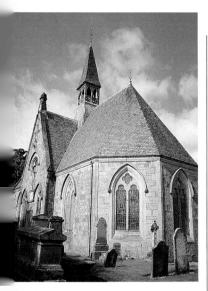

Victorian Luss church, Loch Lomondside

Loch Lomond

Map Ref: 91NN3700

Celebrated in a song which has spread far beyond the bounds of Scotland, Loch Lomond is the largest sheet of inland water in Britain, almost 23 miles from north to south. The northern part of the loch is a narrow cleft between high mountains. The southern part is totally different, fanning out in a spread of richly-wooded islands.

This is recreational water. The tangle of islands makes Loch Lomond an ideal sailing, motor-boating, canoeing, water-skiing and sail-boarding area. Game-fisherman set out to catch salmon, sea trout and brown trout. There is coarse angling, too, for pike and perch, roach and eels, although – as on Loch Eck – little chance to catch the elusive powan, the fresh-water herring.

From the south, Loch Lomond is approached by the A82 from Glasgow. A detour has to be made to reach Balloch, the village at the head of the River Leven, which acts as the gateway to Loch Lomond.

At Balloch the Leven is crowded with boatyards, and this is where many of the loch cruises start. On the east bank is Balloch Park, with woods and meadows and riverside walks. There is a nature trail through the park, a visitor centre, and, hidden away unexpectedly at the heart of it, a quiet walled garden.

The road up the west bank of the Leven leads to a picnic area near Balloch Pier. The *Countess Fiona* runs scheduled cruises up the loch in summer. Alongside are the grounds of Cameron House, now a wildlife park.

The A82 reaches the lochside at Duck Bay, where a bypassed stretch of the main road has been retained as another picnic area. Offshore is Inchmurrin, biggest of Loch Lomond's islands, with a farm and some holiday houses, and a hotel with its own private ferry. The most impressive feature of the view is the wedged summit of Ben Lomond, 3192ft high and the most southerly mountain over 3000ft in Scotland.

Beyond Duck Bay, the A82 goes through the hamlet of Arden, then runs alongside the boundary wall of Rossdhu, seat of the Colquhouns of Luss, who can trace their ownership of the Luss estates in an unbroken line from the 14th century.

Luss itself, down a side-road from the A82, is the picturebook village of Loch Lomondside, mostly Victorian cottages with roses round the doors, and a main street that leads to a shingle bay and a recently rebuilt pier. There is an attractive parish church of 1875, with many earlier relics, on a rise of ground above the sparkling Luss Water. Between the church and the main road is the field where Luss Highland Games are held every July.

On the other side of the A82, a narrow hill road clambers steeply up Glen Luss. It has few parking places but offers long-distance views of the loch and its islands.

The next village on the lochside is Inverbeg. It has a hotel, an art gallery, a camping and caravan site, and a passenger ferry to Rowardennan at the foot of Ben Lomond. Beyond the hotel a side-road leads to Inverbeg youth hostel and then hairpins dizzily uphill into the wilds of Glen Douglas.

Loch Lomond becomes narrower north of Luss. Alongside the 'narrows' of the loch, the A82 twists along a wooded hillside to the road-junction village of Tarbet, built round a typically Victorian hotel.

Another narrow and winding stretch of the A82, through lochside woods, leads to a sharp corner over the bridge at Inveruglas, where generations of travellers have kept a lookout for the tree on the left side 'growing out of a rock'. The bare hills beyond the boundary of the Inveruglas Water are the catchment area for a hydro-electric scheme. Sadly, the huge pipes which bring the water downhill to the turbines of the lochside power station are all too visible. Half a mile north, however, there is a lochside car park with a picnic area and a much more natural viewpoint.

Beyond Inveruglas the main road winds through open country to Ardlui. The West Highland Railway, within earshot from Tarbet, is now more clearly in view. There is a station at Ardlui, caravan and camping sites, and a pier.

Returning to Balloch and taking the A811 north-east towards Drymen leads to the village of Gartocharn. A side-road to the right after Gartocharn Hotel goes to the start of a short but steep footpath to the summit of Duncryne. This hill is a 360-degree viewpoint, but the greatest attraction is the panorama of Loch Lomond, the wooded islands and the mountains piling up on the northern skyline.

A loop road north of Gartocharn leads past the driveway to Ross

View across Loch Lomond to Inversnaid

Loch Maree overlooked by Slioch

Priory, a Georgian mansion house now owned by the University of Strathclyde. Its gardens, bright with rhododendrons and azaleas, are occasionally open to the public. This road also leads to a walker's route into the quiet lochside woods of the Loch Lomond Nature Reserve.

In Drymen, a dead-end road turns off to the left of Balmaha, the main village on the eastern shore of the loch. Balmaha has a busy boatyard, from which visitors can be ferried to the nature reserve island of Inchailloch just offshore. A nature trail has been laid out across its oak-covered hillsides, leading past the ruins of a 12th-century church and churchyard. Passengers are also carried on the mail-boat which sails from Balmaha to the inhabited islands.

From a Forestry Commission car park at Balmaha a gentle walk leads through low-lying plantations. A much steeper route climbs through larch woods to a series of hilltop viewpoints, then down to the water's edge at Balmaha pier.

Northwards, the road wanders past farms, forests and camping and caravan sites among the lochside oakwoods. There are parking and picnic places by the gravelly shore or beside the rocks of some more rugged inlets, and forest trails at Sallochy and Blair.

As well as these out-and-back walks, the eastern shore of Loch Lomond is also on the route of the West Highland Way, Scotland's first long-distance footpath, which heads north all the way to Fort William.

The public road ends at Rowardennan, beside another extensive car park and picnic area among the woodlands at the very foot of Ben Lomond. The main Ben Lomond footpath starts here, and so do other cross-country hikes over the hills to Loch Ard and Aberfoyle.

From Rowardennan the West Highland Way leads north for seven miles to Inversnaid, last of the Loch Lomond villages. Reaching Inversnaid by car is a much more roundabout process, by way of Drymen, Aberfoyle, Loch Ard and Loch Arklet.

Just beyond the west end of Loch Arklet is Garrison of Inversnaid – its name unusually aggressive for just a cluster of farm buildings near a primary school. But there was once a garrison here, a government barracks built in Jacobite days. The soldiers had a hard time of it, though, because Inversnaid was the home of Rob Roy MacGregor, who was not only an outlaw and cattle-raider, but also a sturdy Jacobite supporter.

After the Garrison, a side-road over the Arklet Water leads to a car park with splendid high-level views across Loch Lomond to the

Tumbling waterfall at Inversnaid

mountains of the Arrochar Alps – all genuine peaks with craggy summits which give the best rock-climbing near Glasgow.

Down at the lochside, Inversnaid itself is a tiny hamlet beside an old coaching hotel. It has an almost microscopic harbour from which a ferry sails to the west shore near Tarbet. The tumbling falls of the Snaid Burn are crossed by a high footbridge which leads south on to the Rowardennan stretch of the West Highland Way.

North of Inversnaid, the Way continues across difficult country to Glen Falloch. But Inversnaid does not insist on energetic pursuits. It is also a place to potter around, admiring the mountains, the falls, the harbour and the loch waters lapping against the rocky shore.

AA recommends:

Guesthouses: Arrochoile, Balmaha, *tel.* Balmaha 231
Mid Ross, Arden (farmhouse), *tel.* 655

Loch Maree

Map Ref: 84NG9370

For many well-travelled visitors, this is the most beautiful inland loch in Scotland. Loch Maree has superb mountain scenery in the roadless wilderness north and east. On the south-west side, the mountains start with the 10,500-acre Beinn Eighe National Nature Reserve above the A832 Kinlochewe-Gairloch road.

The reserve's visitor centre at Aultroy is between Kinlochewe and the head of Loch Maree. Two fine nature trails start from a lochside picnic site two miles farther on. One reaches 350ft and the other 1800ft.

The classic low-level view in the district is from Bridge of Grudie, across the loch to the splendidly-proportioned peak of Slioch. Beyond Bridge of Grudie, the road goes briefly inland before coming to the water's edge at the angling centre of Talladale, where the views over the loch, this time, are directly to its scattering of wooded islands. A short forest walk leads to the Victoria Falls, named after a 19th-century royal visit.

At Slattadale, the Forestry Commission has laid out a car park and picnic site. And from here there is also the start of a five-mile cross-country walk, at first by the lochside and then climbing over a pass to finish near Tollie on the Gairloch-Poolewe road.

AA recommends:
Hotels: Kinlochewe, Kinlochewe, I-star, *tel.* 253
Loch Maree, Loch Maree, Talladel, *tel.* Lochmaree 200
Self Catering: Cairn Shiel, Tarridon Road, Kinlochewe, *tel.* Grasmere 259

Unexplorably deep Loch Ness, viewed from above Inverfarigaig

Loch Ness

Map Ref: 87NH5223

Never mind that its peat-dark waters, impenetrable by even the most powerful submarine light, never freeze; that it is more than 20 miles long, is rarely more than a mile in width, and plunges to a greatest recorded depth of almost 1000ft. The single most important statistic about Loch Ness is that its unexplorable depths may be the home of some so-far unidentified 'monster'.

Going north-east along the Great Glen from Fort William, the A82 reaches the head of the loch at Fort Augustus. A bridge in the centre of the village takes the main road over the Caledonian Canal, which joins Loch Ness here. In parkland by the lochside is St Benedict's Abbey, built in the 1880s around a fragment of the Hanoverian fort which gave the village its name. The Abbey is now a boys' school, and guided tours are arranged in the summer.

Also in the village is the Great Glen Exhibition, open daily during the summer. South of Fort Augustus is a golf course, a rare amenity in these parts. Off the main road to the north of the village are Forestry Commission picnic sites and a woodland trail along the banks of the River Oich.

The A82 continues by a quiet bay well known to yachtsmen, trout and salmon fishermen, then runs through lochside woods to Invermoriston, Lewiston and Drumnadrochit. Before Lewiston is the memorial to John Cobb, that most gentlemanly of record-breakers, who was killed on the loch in 1952 in his jet-powered boat *Crusader.*

Also on the lochside is the substantial ruin of the mainly 16th-century Urquhart Castle, once the home of the chiefs of Clan Grant. It is open to the public as an Ancient Monument.

In Lewiston, a side-road to the left leads towards a forest walk through oakwoods to the waterfalls on the Divach Burn. At Drumnadrochit, the Loch Ness Centre, open daily, includes a hotel, the Highland Kilt Museum and the Loch Ness Monster Exhibition.

From Drumnadrochit the A82 follows the lochside and then the River Ness into Inverness. It is a modern road, although without the benefit of a dual carriageway. A more dramatic drive from Fort Augustus is to take the A862 which turns right before St Benedict's Abbey, then climbs steeply over the hills to Loch Tarff and Whitebridge. Beyond Whitebridge the B852 turns off to the left near a lonely church, winding down through birchwoods and heather to the two-part village of Foyers.

Opposite the post office in Upper Foyers, a footpath leads sharply down through the woods to a viewpoint looking directly across to the Falls of Foyers, as they plummet into a dark rock pool below. Lower Foyers is down a minor road to the left, and overlooks the shore of Loch Ness.

The unexpected size of these twin hillside villages is explained by the fact that, in the 1890s, Britain's first aluminium works was established here. Power was generated by a pioneering industrial hydro-electric scheme which diverted the waters of

St Benedict's Abbey, based on a Hanoverian fort, is now a boys' school

Remains of Urquhart Castle, Loch Ness

the falls. Curiously enough, the abbot of St Benedict's had set up a smaller-scale generating scheme here just a few years earlier.

The aluminium factory closed in 1967, but in 1975 the North of Scotland Hydro-Electric Board's new pumped-storage system started feeding current to the Highland Grid. The modern power station is on the water's edge, just north of the old aluminium works.

Beyond Foyers is Inverfarigaig, a hamlet on a ledge above the loch. To the right, the first side-road leads into the constricted Pass of Inverfarigaig. Forest plantations climb steeply on one side, facing beetling rocky crags across a deep-set burn. Farigaig Forest Centre, in the Pass, is the start of a strenuous forest trail.

The second road to the right off the B852 is one of the most astonishing in the Highlands. It suddenly corkscrews up a dizzy hillside of birches, heather and rocky outcrops, emerging after six formidable hairpin bends in half a mile near a magnificent viewpoint high above Loch Ness, from which an imaginative visitor can ponder over the mysteries far below.

Self Catering: For a selection of self catering accommodation, please consult the AA guide *Holiday Homes, Cottages and Apartments in Britain.*
Guesthouse: Lewiston Arms, Lewiston, Drumnadrochit (inn), tel. 225
Garage: Lewiston (J A Menzies & Sons), Drumnadrochit, tel. 212 (day), 502 (night)

Loch Tay

Map Ref: 92NN7040

Fifteen miles long, surrounded by hillsides and forests, Loch Tay has the A827 from Killin to Kenmore above its northern shore, and a pleasant minor road taking the southern route. At the head of the loch, Killin is well known for its dramatic south-western approach, as the A827 runs alongside the rock-slabs, whirlpools, pine-clad islands and miniature cascades of the Falls of Dochart, before crossing the River Dochart into the main street.

Killin has the air of a mountain village, dominated from the north-east by the peaks of the Tarmachans and, beyond them, the 3984ft bulk of Ben Lawers. It has a good range of hotels, boarding-houses and shops. Climbers, hill-walkers, golfers, dinghy-sailors, canoeists and anglers come here and enjoy the facilities. Loch Tay, the River Tay and all its main tributaries are famous salmon and trout waters.

At the north end of the village, just before the A827 crosses the Bridge of Lochay, there is a side-road to the left. It goes up the glen to the Falls of Lochay, behind the power station which acts as the control centre for the vast Breadalbane hydro-electric scheme. At the junction beyond the falls, the left turn makes for the dead-end of upper Glen Lochay. The right turn leads back down to the A827 as it begins a winding climb which takes it higher above Loch Tay.

Just after Edramucky Bridge, a side-road turns steeply uphill to tackle the pass between the Tarmachans and Ben Lawers. On the right of the climb is the National Trust for Scotland's Ben Lawers visitor centre. This area is famous for its wide range of alpine plants in very varied habitats. The centre, which has displays on the geology and natural history of the mountain from the ice age onwards, is open from April to September.

At Fearnan, the A827 comes down to the lochside. A side-road to the left leads towards the entrance to Glen Lyon – the longest glen in Scotland – and the village of Fortingall, well-known for the ancient yew in the parish churchyard, perhaps the oldest living thing in Britain, and for the legend that Pontius Pilate was born here while his father was helping to patrol the borders of the Roman Empire.

Past the lochside picnic site below the larchwoods at Dalerb, as the A827 bends right into Kenmore, another minor road to the left leads towards the forest walks on Drummond Hill.

Kenmore is one of the most beautifully situated villages in Scotland. Rustic cottages line the short street from the parish church overlooking Loch Tay to the imposing gateway to the grounds of Taymouth Castle, once the seat of the Earls and Marquesses of

Breadalbane. The village inn was built in 1572 and claims to be the oldest in Scotland. Robert Burns visited it during his Highland tour in 1787, and verses he wrote about Kenmore are preserved on a chimney-piece.

Busiest day of the year in Kenmore is the 15 January, the ceremonial opening of the Tay salmon season. The River Tay, which flows eastwards out of the loch under a well-preserved bridge dating from 1774, continues past an 18-hole parkland golf course towards the rapids of Grandtully.

The other road from Killin to Kenmore, along the south side of the loch, goes through Ardeonaig and Ardtalnaig – two more angling centres – and the one-time mill village of Acharn.

A farm track which goes uphill beside the rebuilt mill provides a pleasant walk to the hidden Falls of Acharn. These are reached by a tunnel built through a ridge of ground to the left of the track. Inside the tunnel, the right fork leads to a well-placed belvedere (a raised turret) looking directly across a heavily-wooded glen to the falls.

Ben Lawers and Loch Tay in a region famed for a range of alpine plants

In Victorian days, when visitors were escorted here, the idea was that the guide, walking politely behind them, would slip along the left-hand fork and suddenly reappear, with fiendish yells, leaping on to the viewpoint wall. Few visitors escaped without a moment of terror that the wild Highlanders were coming to get them!

AA recommends:
Garage: Lix Toll, Lix Toll, Killin, *tel.* 280

The white waters of Dochart Falls

Loch Torridon

Map Ref: 86NG7563

While there will always be arguments about personal tastes in landscape, there is little doubt that the supreme example of mountain and sea-loch scenery on the mainland of Scotland is around Loch Torridon and Upper Loch Torridon in Wester Ross, with the subsidiary inlets of Loch Shieldaig and Loch Diabaig.

The major northern peaks – 3232ft at Beinn Alligin, 2995ft at Beinn Dearg and right up to 3456ft at the highest point of the seven summits of Liathach – have had 750 million years to mature. Torridonian sandstone is one of the oldest rocks in the world, and provides excellent mountaineering.

The entire area of Liathach and Beinn Alligin, together with the southern slopes of Beinn Dearg, are now owned by the National Trust for Scotland, whose Torridon estate covers more than 16,000 acres of the Highlands.

From the south, the A896 from Lochcarron picks its way through Glen Shieldaig to reach tidal water at the head of Loch Shieldaig. A turning to the left is the start of the adventurous 'new' road round the northern tip of the Applecross peninsula, connecting previously remote villages like Ardheslaig and Kenmore, Arinacrinachd, Fearnbeg and Fearnmore.

Above Loch Shieldaig, the A896 skirts the attractively situated village of the same name, whose whitewashed houses look out to the pinewood of Shieldaig Island, another Trust property. Then it sweeps round the shoulder of a hill to follow a stunningly beautiful route above the south shore of Upper Loch Torridon. This stretch of the A896 was completed in 1963 to close the so-called Balgy Gap, across the river that chatters down from Loch Damh in the southern hills.

From Shieldaig to Annat, the main road passes above the gorgeous rocky

Something for all tastes in Lochinver

and wooded bays indenting the southern shore. But the near-at-hand view is only the foreground for the glorious mountain skyline across the loch.

Beyond the crofts of Annat, the A896 heads east up Glen Torridon and a minor road turns off left towards Inveralligin and Diabaig. Beside the junction is the Trust's Torridon visitor centre, open from June to September. A short distance along the Diabaig road is the purpose-built Torridon youth hostel, a favourite stop for climbers and hill-walkers.

Torridon village looks to be precariously sited, below the great scree-slopes of Liathach. For a time, the road beyond it hugs the lochside, but then it turns sharply uphill above the pinewoods of Torridon House to the bridge over the ravine of the Coire Mhic Nobuil burn. A car park at the bridge is the starting point for some exhilarating walks on glen footpaths, which give the comparatively low-level explorer a fine view of the peaks, corries and pinnacles which are the playground of rock-climbers. The main path runs through the pines on the east bank of the burn, past waterfalls.

Now running high above the loch, with extensive views to the west and south, the Diabaig road comes to a junction where a side-turning to the left dips down to the spread-out lochside village of Inveralligin. It has a grassy parking space near the water's edge and striking views across the loch to the end-on ridges of Beinn Shieldaig and Beinn Damh.

Back on the high road, past the turn-off to the crofting settlement of Wester Alligin, there is a steep, narrow and blind-cornered assault on the Bealach na Gaoithe – the Pass of the Wind. Over the pass, which has a viewpoint on the summit, the road skirts two freshwater lochs and then plunges down to the scattered crofts and houses of Diabaig, on a gradient which reaches 1 in 3½ – the steepest public-road hill in Scotland.

The climb, however, is well worth the effort. Diabaig is set in a towering rocky amphitheatre round its own dramatic sea-loch. There is a car park by the pier, which is itself built up of multi-coloured rocks. Picnickers may have to fend off the attentions of the occasional well-mannered, but persistent, goat.

But perhaps Diabaig is best in the

Torridon peaks, great for climbers

Rock formation at Tarlair, Macduff

Top right: Macduff and its harbour

Macduff

Map Ref: 89NJ7064

Macduff, on the opposite side of the Deveron estuary from Banff, is the main fishing port on this stretch of coast, as well as a holiday resort. It has a fleet of seine-net fishing boats and its own quayside market.

While the harbour activity can be watched at close quarters, there is a higher-level viewpoint in front of the hillside Doune church, beside a massive anchor claimed to be from a wrecked ship of the Spanish Armada.

At the foot of the cliffs east of the town, the open-air Tarlair swimming pool has been a popular bathing resort for many years.

Like Banff, Macduff offers angling on the Deveron, and a pleasant walk through Montcoffer Wood, high above the river, meets up with the west-bank path from Duff House at the Bridge of Alvah.

evening, when in the long, lingering West Highland dusk, the sun sets in a blaze of red and orange over Applecross, Rona and the northern peaks of Skye.

Lochinver

Map Ref: 84NC0922

Although it is the home port of a commercial fishing fleet, an angling centre and the base for boat trips to the islands of Enard Bay, Lochinver is dominated by the inland deer-forest mountains of Assynt. From the west side of the village at Baddidarrach, the view over Lochinver and the houses along the shore road has the 'sugar loaf' summit of Suilven looming on the skyline.

From Ledmore to Lochinver, the main A837 is a modern road through wild and timeless scenery. The mountains of Quinag and Canisp tower over it, as it goes through the angling resort of Inchnadamph and along the north side of Loch Assynt. There is a 3200-acre nature reserve at Inchnadamph, and the limestone beds on which this prodigious mountain landscape is based are shown clearly on the face of the 300ft cliffs at Stronchrubie, by the roadside before the village.

The main road into Lochinver from the east is a well engineered one, but a more dramatic approach –

from the driver's point of view – is the narrow and twisting minor road from the south. Around Inverkirkaig it gives widespread seaward views.

AA recommends:

Self Catering: Lochinver Holiday Lodges, 33 Strathan, *tel.* 282

Guesthouses: Ardglas, *tel.* 257
Hillcrest, Badnaban, *tel.* 391

Haggis

Contrary to popular belief south of the border, haggis is not shot seasonally on the moors; this greatest of Scottish savouries is the result of painstaking culinary expertise.

Although generally regarded as Scotland's national dish, haggis was, in fact, also common in England until the 18th century; thereafter its popularity waned. Was it perhaps that the Sassenachs came to learn of its innermost secrets? It has to be said that the ingredients of what Robert Burns described as the 'great chieftain o' the pudden race' do not make pleasant reading for the squeamish.

Haggis is made from the heart, lungs and liver of a sheep, all finely chopped, combined with suet, onions, oatmeal, black pepper, salt, herbs and either vinegar or lemon juice. The mixture is sewn up in a sheep's cleaned and pre-boiled stomach bag and then boiled for about three hours. The bag has to be pricked here and there with a darning needle as soon as it starts to swell to prevent it from exploding — with the obvious consequences.

The tasty dish is served hot from the pot with neeps and tatties (turnips and potatoes) and, traditionally, washed down with neat whisky. On festive occasions, such as St Andrew's Night celebrations, the haggis is majestically piped into the dining room by a resplendently-clad Scottish piper.

Mallaig

Map Ref: 86NM6796

This is the end of the Road to the Isles. Mallaig is the terminal for the car-ferry to Armadale on Skye. Other ferries leave for the islands of Rum, Eigg, Muck and Canna, and for Inverie on Loch Nevis, the only village in the remote district of Knoydart, which has no road connection with the rest of mainland Scotland. Mallaig is also the western terminus of the West Highland Railway. The bustling fishing-boat quays are well worth visiting.

The Road to the Isles – the winding A830 – is steeped in the story of the Jacobite Risings. At Glenfinnan, a monument commemorates the raising of the Jacobite standard in 1745. There is a National Trust for Scotland visitor centre, open daily from April to October. Loch nan Uamh is where Bonnie Prince Charlie first landed on Scottish soil, and also where, the Stuart cause defeated, he finally sailed away.

Two villages south of Mallaig are holiday resorts. Arisaig is built round a series of bays, with breathtaking views over the sea to the mountains of Skye and Rum. Morar is famous for its white sandy beaches. Loch Morar, behind the village, is the deepest inland water in Britain – and the reputed home of Morag, a mysterious creature not unlike the monster of Loch Ness.

The Mearns

Map Ref: 89NO6274

Between the foothills of the Grampians and the North Sea, the heart of the Mearns is a landscape of rich farmlands and wooded estates. Laurencekirk is the main, but small-scale, inland market town, once famous for the snuff-boxes which are now valuable collectors' pieces.

On the edge of the hills, close to the line of the Highland Boundary Fault, Fettercairn has a grand and unexpected Gothic archway

Quiet reflection in Mallaig harbour

Right: Drumlithie village and steeple

entrance, commemorating the visit of Queen Victoria and Prince Albert in 1861.

North of the village, the mansion-house of Fasque, home of the Gladstones, is occasionally open to visitors. Victoria's prime minister was one of this family.

Auchenblae is a hillside village with a pleasant riverbank 'den', a golf course, the preserved ruin of a 13th-century chapel and access to the forest walks in Drumtochty Glen.

Glenbervie churchyard is notable for the graves of Robert Burn's Mearns relations. Nearby, Drumlithie has an elegant little 18th-century steeple which once tolled the handloom weavers' hours.

A few miles down the winding course of the Bervie Water, the out-of-the-way parish church of St Ternan's Arbuthnott is one of the architectural glories of the Mearns, dating in part from 1242 and very carefully restored.

From the south, the coastal settlements start with St Cyrus, which has a cliff-edge nature reserve and a salmon-netting station. Johnshaven harbour now concentrates on shellfish, but white-fish auctions are still held every working day on the quayside at Gourdon, which also has facilities for sea angling.

Inverbervie has a figurehead memorial to the local man Hercules Linton, designer of the famous 19th-

century tea-clipper *Cutty Sark*.

Kineff's historic church was where the crown jewels of Scotland were hidden for years from Cromwell's troops. And gallery-goers all over Scotland know the clifftop village of Catterline, above a fishing and watersports base, thanks to the landscape painting of Joan Eardley.

AA recommends:

Guesthouse: Ringwood, Fordoun (farmhouse), *tel.* Auchenblane 313

Moidart

Map Ref: 90NM7075

At Inverailort on the Glenfinnan to Mallaig road the A861 turns south towards Kinlochmoidart. The beautiful seaward views from it were out of bounds to motorists until the 1960s, when the present road was built to replace an existing bridle-path.

A side-road to the right of Glenuig leads to the sheltered tidal bay of Samalaman. From there, a footpath goes over a pass to the one-time crofting settlement of Smearisary, looking out over the sea to Eigg.

From Glenuig the A861 goes over the shoulder of a hill and down again to Kinlochmoidart. Bonnie Prince Charlie stayed at Kinlochmoidart House in 1745, on his way to the raising of the Jacobite standard at Glenfinnan.

Midway down Loch Moidart, reached by a side-road off the A861, the ruin of Castle Tioram is one of the great sights of the coast. It was the fortress of the MacDonalds of Clanranald, built on a rock at the end of a natural causeway, which allows it to be reached on foot – except at high tide.

Sunset at St Cyrus nature reserve

Whisky

A characteristic feature of many Highland valleys — in Speyside, Glenlivet, Perthshire and elsewhere — are the whitewashed buildings of malt whisky distilleries, with the pagoda-like roofs of their barley-drying kilns. Although there are many blended whiskies, connoisseurs prefer single malts, each of which comes from one particular distillery.

No two malt whiskies are identical, even when produced in distilleries only half a mile apart; and the taste, thanks to the water from the hill burns and springs, cannot be duplicated anywhere else in the world. Incidentally, this is the only case where the adjective Scotch is used instead of Scottish.

The first record of whisky distilling in Scotland is dated 1494. Imposition of excise duty in 1644 led to nearly two centuries of determined and profitable smuggling. The business settled down to its modern form after a more reasonable Act of Parliament in 1823.

There are more than 100 malt whisky distilleries in the Highlands and Islands. Many of them offer guided tours to demonstrate the carefully-timed processes involved in producing what Gaelic speakers call *uisge-beatha* — the water of life. Six of such distilleries lie on the so-called 'Whisky Trail'; this is a signposted road tour some 70 miles long. Allow about an hour for each distillery visit, but make sure that only car passengers do the sampling.

Casks of maturing whisky, Dufftown

Montrose

Map Ref: 93NO7157

This versatile Angus town spreads north from docks at the narrow mouth of the River South Esk – busy with cargo ships, fishing boats and North Sea oil work; but immediately inland the river has created a vast tidal basin which dries out almost completely at low water. Montrose Basin is a nature reserve, a fine place for observing pinkfoot and greylag geese, wigeon and redshank.

The town centre has many attractive older buildings, some of them originally town mansions of wealthy landed families. East of the main street there is a district with a notably spacious and elegant air.

Montrose museum is strong on relics of the old whaling industry, Pictish stones and locally-gathered collections of fossils and agates.

The built-up area does not encroach on the Links, where golf courses are laid out behind the dunes which border the long stretches of sandy beach.

AA recommends:
Guesthouses: Linksgate, 11 Dorward Road, *tel.* 72273
Muirshade of Gallery (farmhouse), *tel.* Northwaterbridge 209

Nairn

Map Ref: 85NH8756

With its situation beside the sea, its natural links-land turf, and one of the mildest and driest climates in Scotland, it is not really surprising that Nairn developed into a well-known golfing resort. The main part of the town, however, is built back from the Moray Firth, around the A96 Inverness to Forres road. There are walks by the shore and along the banks of the River Nairn. The Constabulary Garden, open daily from May to September, is a pleasant town-centre retreat.

At Viewfield House there is a local-history museum with a display on the Battle of Culloden; and the days when Nairn was a premier fishing port are recalled in the old Fishertown.

South-west of Nairn, off the B9090, Cawdor Castle is the most famous stately home in the district. Macbeth was Thane of Cawdor in Shakespeare's play, but the existing building is of much later date. The 14th-century castle, home of the present-day Earl of Cawdor, is open daily from May to October. Attractions include not only tours of the castle itself, in its fine setting among gardens and woodland on the banks of a rocky burn, but also a network of varied nature trails.

AA recommends:
Hotel: Clifton, 1-rosette, 2-star, *tel.* 53119
Guesthouses: Greenlawns Private Hotel, 13 Seafield Street, *tel.* 52738
Sandown Farmhouse, Sandown Farm Lane, *tel.* 54745
Sunny Brae, Marine Road, *tel.* 52309

Newburgh

Map Ref: 93NO2318

Anglers often come to Newburgh to fish the tidal waters of the narrow and winding estuary of the River Ythan for sea trout and salmon. There is also a peninsula golf course at the start of the 12-mile stretch of beach, extending all the way south to Aberdeen.

Across the Ythan is one of the most remarkable nature reserves in Scotland. The Sands of Forvie reserve – linked with another which includes the estuary itself – covers a huge area of sand dunes, cliffs and tidal shore.

This is Britain's largest nesting site for eider ducks, and there are also great numbers of geese, waders and terns.

A waymarked path leads over tussocky heathland to the ruined parish church of Forvie, all that remains above ground of a village abandoned to the encroaching sandhills, and then follows the shore north towards the village of Collieston.

AA recommends:
Hotel: Udny Arms, Main Street, 1-rosette, 2-star, *tel.* 444

Montrose has many fine buildings. These are to the east of town centre

McCaig's tower, built to provide work

Oban

Map Ref: 90NM8630

Built round a curving bay, sheltered by the long island of Kerrera from the open waters of the Firth of Lorn, Oban is a holiday resort with many seafront hotels, as well as a trading and transport centre. It is the terminus of the West Highland railway from Glasgow, and the Railway Pier, busy with fishing boats unloading their catches, is the start of many car-ferry routes, to Mull, Coll and Tiree, Barra and South Uist, Colonsay and the nearer island of Lismore. There are cruises to Iona, and local boat-hirers run excursions to smaller islets which are breeding grounds of seals.

South of the harbour, there are walks on Pulpit Hill, past the wooded grounds of well-placed Victorian villas to a viewpoint on the summit. Directly inland, the skyline is marked by McCaig's tower, a folly built in the 1890s to provide work at a time of depression. This near-replica of the Colosseum in Rome is a place for marvellous westward views.

Oban Bay is a fine sailing area. Sea-anglers have marks off Kerrera. Loch and river fishermen have plenty of choice inland, such as the trout and salmon beats of Loch Scamadale and the River Euchar which flows from it to join the sea at Kilninver, on the A816 south of the town.

Oban has an 18-hole golf course in a wooded setting in Glencruitten. Shinty is a favourite game here. And Oban Highland Games – otherwise known as the Arlgyllshire Gathering – are the main sporting and social event of the summer.

North of the bay, a road above the shore passes picnic sites among the pines and leads to Ganavan Sands. This is Oban's swimming and sun-bathing centre, with an abundance of parking space and a caravan site nearby.

The easiest island to reach from Oban is Kerrera, a fine place for a day's outing. Along Gallanach Road there is parking space beside the jetty from which the ferry makes its five-minute crossing. A circular walk of about six miles can be followed on Kerrera, on farm tracks and footpaths, past the ruins of the 16th-century Gylen Castle. The wild scenery and the sense of away-from-it-all are matched by the varied seaward views.

South of Oban, a turning off the A816 near Kilniver leads on to the B844 which crosses the high-arched Clachan Bridge – optimistically called 'the bridge over the Atlantic' – up to the island of Seil. Ellanbeich on the west coast is a one-time slate-quarriers' village turned into a neatly whitewashed holiday centre. The sheltered garden of An Cala is open on Monday and Thursday afternoons from April to September. A ferry crosses to the smaller slate island of Easdale, which has its own folk museum.

Back on the mainland, beyond the golf course at Glencruitten, a minor road to the south goes alongside Loch Nell to rejoin the A816 near the head of Loch Feochan. Farther east, the road through Glen Lonan passes Barguillean, where a lochside garden is open daily from April to October.

Northwards, another country road leads to Connel, on the south shore of Loch Etive at the Falls of Lora – the tide-race under the former railway bridge which takes the A826 into the districts of Benderloch and Barcaldine. Off the A826 there are forest walks, one leading to the 1010ft summit of Beinn Lora.

The Sea Life Centre, before the village of Barcaldine, is open from April to October. Tanks contain displays of all kinds of fish, from rays and octopus to turbot and eels. And a twice-daily attraction is the seal feeding in the open-air pool.

Turning off to the right at Barcaldine, the B845 goes up through the forest plantations of Gleann Salach then down to the shore of Loch Etive and an unexpectedly industrial-looking quarry village.

A very pleasant minor road from Inveresragan on the B845 wanders along the north shore of Loch Etive, back to the bridge at Connel. It passes Ardchattan Priory. This is a private house, based on a ruined 13th-century Benedictine priory, and can be visited on occasional summer Sundays.

The main attraction at Ardchattan, however, is the garden, open daily from April to October. Its herbaceous borders and flowering shrubs are a reminder that there are attractive miniature landscapes around Oban, as well as the grander-scale mountains, forests, sea-lochs and islands offshore.

AA recommends:
Hotel: Lancaster, Corran Esplanade, 2-star, tel. 62587
Self Catering: For a selection of self catering accommodation, please consult the AA guide *Holiday Homes, Cottages and Apartments in Britain.*
Guesthouses: For a selection of guesthouses, please consult the AA guide *Guesthouses, Farmhouses and Inns in Britain.*

The gleaming still house at Glen Garioch distillery in Oldmeldrum

Garages: J Cook Motor Engineers, Lochavoulin Industrial Estate, tel. 64463 (day), 63987 (night)
Mogil Motors, Soroba Road, tel. 63061 (day), 63087 (night)
Struthers, Breadalbane Place, tel. 63066

Oldmeldrum

Map Ref: 82NJ8027

A high-set town in the heart of extensive farming country, Oldmeldrum lies on the borders of the old provinces of Formartine and Garioch and has an interesting conservation area around its Market Square. Glengarioch distillery on the outskirts is open to visitors, and has a notable reputation for energy conservation – its glasshouses producing a rich crop of tomatoes every year.

Five miles east, the National Trust for Scotland's splendid Great Garden of Pitmedden has been restored to its formal 17th-century style, and some of the estate buildings have been converted into a Museum of Farming Life.

North-east of Oldmeldrum is another major Trust property – the handsomely-furnished Haddo House, completed in 1732 for the Earl of Aberdeen. It is well known for its music-society concerts.

The mansion house stands at the edge of Haddo Country Park, where nature trails explore the varied woodlands, the parkland, and the edges of a lake where tufted duck, moorhens and swans cruise in the summer.

Of the nearby villages, Tarves is a 19th-century conservation area in its own right; Methlick, with an imposing Victorian parish church, is an angling centre for the Upper Ythan.

AA recommends:
Garage: Meldrum Motors, 3 Market Square, tel. 2247

Perth

Map Ref: 92NO1123

At its heart, Perth is a Georgian town, although St John's Kirk dates from the 15th century. A fiery sermon preached here by John Knox in May 1559 sparked off the Reformation in Scotland.

The South Inch and the North Inch have been public parks since 1377. On the North Inch are playing fields, a golf course and the ground of the Perthshire Cricket Club. The very modern Bell's Sports Centre stands beside Balhousie Castle, the Black Watch regimental museum. And within yards of them is the Douglas Garden, set out in memory of the Perthshire botanist David Douglas.

Other places to visit include the art gallery and museum; the National Trust for Scotland's Branklyn Garden, open daily from March to October; and the meandering woodland walks on the summit of Kinnoull Hill.

Within the town boundaries there is salmon fishing on the Tay. And one of Perth's golf courses is curiously situated – on an island in the middle of the river, reached only by a footpath on the bridge which carries the main railway line to Dundee.

North of the town, Scone Palace and its grounds – which include a pinetum and a woodland garden – are open daily from Easter to October. The present house was completed in 1808, but from the 9th century until Charles II was crowned in 1651, this was the coronation place of the Scottish kings.

Pitlochry

Map Ref: 92NN9458

Set in one of the most beautiful valleys in the Central Highlands, Pitlochry is a holiday resort of hotels and boarding houses, with camping and caravan sites nearby, facilities for golf, angling and boating, an indoor sports centre and any number of exhilarating hill and forest walks.

The North of Scotland Hydro-Electric Board's reservoir of Loch Faskally has winding banks clothed in natural woodland. On the east side of the loch, a Forestry Commission

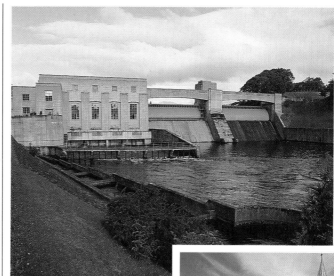

trail goes through the woodland garden of a former private estate and round an ornamental lake.

At the south end of the loch there is a fish pass, with an observation room from which salmon can be seen battling their way upstream.

Pitlochry Festival Theatre has graduated from its original marquee of 1951 to a modern, purpose-built £2 million building – but it is still very much Scotland's 'theatre in the hills'.

Top: Pitlochry salmon-ladder bypasses the swirling River Tummel

Above: St John's Kirk, Perth

West Highland Way

Opened in 1980, this was the first of Scotland's long-distance footpaths, running for 95 miles from Milngavie, north of Glasgow, to finish at Fort William, under the shoulder of Ben Nevis.

The first part of the route is through farmed and wooded country, using footpaths, minor roads and the line of the old Blane Valley Railway. Then a hill walk takes the Way by magnificent viewpoints to Balmaha on Loch Lomond. From there it goes through the lochside oakwoods to Rowardennan, and continues north on forest roads and paths to Inversnaid.

There is tougher walking through Glen Falloch, easier going in Strathfillan, and then the route spends much of its time on an old military road through the mountains from Tyndrum by Bridge of Orchy and Inveroran. On the stretch from Inveroran by way of Ba Bridge to Kingshouse Hotel on the edge of Glencoe, there are far views eastwards over Rannoch Moor.

This is a lonely and exposed part of the route, as is the tough stage from Glencoe over the Devil's Staircase to Kinlochleven. The climb from Kinlochleven leads to the final crossing, by hill-tracks and forest roads, to Glen Nevis.

A huddle of houses at Kinlochleven

Queen's View

Map Ref: 92NN8360

Queen's View, lying north-west of Pitlochry, beside the B8019 which runs along the north side of Loch Tummel, is one of the most famous viewpoints in Scotland, and was so christened after Queen Victoria admired the view on an excursion in 1866. There is a Forestry Commission information centre open from Easter to September on one side of the road, and, on the other, forest walks climbing to more viewpoints, an excavated ring fort of the 8th or 9th century, and a reconstructed 18th-century farm village.

Beyond Loch Tummel is Loch Rannoch. The Rannoch Forest walks, based on the woodland picnic site at Carie on the south side, include short walks around the Carie Burn, and a longer five-mile trail through plantations of pine and larch, birch and spruce into the hills overlooking the loch.

AA recommends:
Hotel: Killiecrankie, Killiecrankie, I-rosette, 2-star, *tel.* Pitlochry 3220
Self Catering: Old Faskally Chalets, Killiecrankie, *tel.* Pitlochry 3436
Guesthouse: Dalnasgadh House, Killiecrankie, *tel.* 3237

Royal Deeside

Map Ref: 89NO3095

Of all the rivers in Britain, the Dee rises highest in the mountains, bubbling up from the Wells of Dee, more than 4000ft above sea level near Einich Cairn in the Cairngorms. From there it plunges down a cliff-edge into the narrow pass of the Lairig Ghru and, gathering tributaries from either side, descends into that area of pinewoods, larch and birch and juniper, rocks and tumbling waters which make up the classic Deeside view.

The landscape of the Braemar to Ballater stretch of the Dee takes in fields along the valley floor, plantations and natural woodlands sweeping up to heathery grouse moors and deer forest country above, and a remote mountain horizon. But what has made it most famous is Balmoral Castle at the heart of an extensive estate, the Royal Family's Highland home.

Queen Victoria and Prince Albert first rented the old Balmoral Castle in 1848. Four years later, Prince Albert bought the property for £31,500. He commissioned the Aberdeen architect William Smith to design a replacement castle of local Glen Gelder granite. Many of the Prince's own ideas were

incorporated in the layout. Victoria and Albert were welcomed to the new castle on 7 September 1855. The future of Royal Deeside was assured.

Opposite the little hamlet of Crathie on the A93 Aberdeen to Braemar road, the B976 crosses the Dee and then turns back along the south bank towards Ballater. The main entrance to the castle is at the corner after the bridge. Visitors are welcome to the grounds and gardens, and to an exhibition in the castle ballroom, on weekdays from May to July when the Royal Family is not in residence. Cars should be parked on the Crathie side of the bridge.

Crathie is often jammed with sightseers when the Royal Family attends the little parish church. The present church, which is open to visitors, dates only from 1895, and because the sparsely populated parish found it hard to gather enough money for the building, a fund-raising bazaar was held in the Balmoral grounds, approved by the 74 year-old Queen Victoria, with members of her family helping to run the stalls.

The centrepiece of the upper part of the valley is the splendidly situated village of Braemar. Members of the Royal Family usually attend the Highland Gathering held there every September. Tens of thousands of spectators throng the games field, to watch the races, the piping and dancing competitions, and the field events such as tossing the massive Braemar caber.

Braemar's Invercauld Arms Hotel is built on the exact site where the Earl of Mar unfurled the Old Pretender's standard, to start the 1715 Jacobite Rising. On lower ground beside the A93, where the Clunie Water which rises in the winter flows into the Dee, Braemar Castle was a Jacobite stronghold, then a government barracks, before being taken over again in the 1830s as the home of the Farquharsons of Invercauld. It is open to the public from May to October.

A less dramatic house to look out for in Braemar is the cottage on the Glenshee road where, in 1881, Robert Louis Stevenson wrote *Treasure Island.*

Braemar is an excellent walking centre. From a car park near the top of Chapel Brae, footpaths meander along the lower slopes of Morrone hill. The birch and juniper woods here are included in a National Nature Reserve.

The minor road which heads west from Braemar, along the south bank of the Dee through the hamlet of Inverey, then turns back over the bridge at the Linn of Dee to finish at Allanaquoich. It is a most attractive drive and also leads to many fine walks.

The Princess Walk from Inverey wanders through woodland to the waterfall at the Linn of Corriemulzie. At the Linn of Dee, the river thrashes

Loch Tummel as seen from Queen's View

A superb setting of Balmoral Castle, the Royal Family's Highland home

Old bridge over the Water of Tanar

and crashes down a rocky chasm crossed by a road bridge which Queen Victoria opened in 1857. On the road back along the north bank, another bridge crosses the tributary Lui Water near a series of waterfalls in the pinewoods. And the public road ends at Allanaquoich, where the swirling action of the Quoich Water has scoured out curious rock formations, such as the Earl of Mar's Punchbowl.

Back in Braemar itself, there is an 18-hole golf course beside the Clunie Water. Permits for salmon fishing in the Dee, at its best from May to July, are available from local hotels. In the heart of the Deeside deer forests, several village shops specialise in horn and woodwork.

If Braemar is the most notable place on Royal Deeside upriver from Balmoral, the first place of

importance downstream is Ballater, a neatly planned little town of granite houses and hotels, laid out in a grid pattern of streets at the end of the 18th century. It was built to provide accommodation for the visitors who flocked to sample the spa water of Pannanich Wells, still available today at a hotel on the B976 about two miles east of the town.

Ballater is in a sheltered situation, between a long bend on the River Dee and the steep-sided, isolated hill of Craigendarroch – the crag of the oak trees. Well-maintained footpaths circle the natural woodlands of Craigendarroch to reach an open-summit viewpoint.

Other walks from Ballater are across the bridge over the Dee and up the steeply wooded slopes of Craig Coillich, and along the Old Line – a cancelled extension of the Deeside Railway from Ballater towards Braemar – which starts at the riverside golf course and follows a ledge above the Dee towards Bridge of Gairn. The railway closed on the east side of Ballater in 1966, and four miles of the old track-bed to Cambus o'May have been turned into a footpath and bridleway.

South-west of Ballater, a minor road climbs into the hills of Glen Muick, which, together with Loch Muick and the granite pinnacles of Lochnagar, forms a massive nature reserve controlled by the Scottish Wildlife Trust and Balmoral estate.

There is a visitor centre near the foot of the loch.

Although the A93 curls south to take in Ballater, the short link road B972, avoiding the town, provides the most spectacular motoring landscapes in the district. It runs along the bottom of the precipitous Pass of Ballater.

As the A93 continues east by Cambus o'May and on to the moorland around Dinnet, it leaves the strictly Highland part of Royal Deeside. Muir of Dinnet is a National Nature Reserve, a wide expanse of heather, oakwood, birch, rowan and pines around Loch Davan and Loch Kinord. The Burn o'Vat, which flows into Loch Kinord from the west, is named after the huge rocky cauldron. A car park and picnic site have been laid out near The Vat on the A97.

There is gliding to watch on the south side of the A93 at Dinnet. Farther along the main road is the Victorian village of Aboyne, in a wooded setting with granite cottages and villas surrounding an extensive green, where the Aboyne Games are held every September.

Across the Dee from Aboyne, a right turn along the B976 leads to Glentanar estate, where a visitor centre is open from April to September. It features a wildlife and land-use exhibition. Outside, there are pleasant woodland walks and a nature trail. Here in this side-valley, once again, are elements of the classic Royal Deeside landscape – a backdrop of hills with pinewoods, heather and a river tumbling through a lovely glen.

Blackhouse croft museum at Luib

Skye

Map Ref: 86NG5030

The largest of Scotland's islands, Skye has a wild and mountainous interior, where the peaks, ridges and pinnacles of the Cuillin Hills are among the finest rock-climbing areas in Europe. The coastline, with all its indentations, is said to stretch for almost a thousand miles. In any description of Skye, take for granted a multiplicity of magnificent sea and mountain views.

The shortest sea-crossing to Skye is by car-ferry from Kyle of Lochalsh to Kyleakin, which takes its name from the Norse King Haakon. He sailed through this narrow strait on his way to defeat at the Battle of Largs in 1263.

Kyle House gardens, beside the A850 as it leaves the village, are notable for their flowering shrubs and splendid coastal views. They are open to the public from May to August. Just offshore is Kyleakin Island. It was the home in 1968–9 of the author-naturalist Gavin Maxwell, after his original home *Camusfearna* on the mainland was burned down.

A side-road to the left goes up lonely Glen Arroch then dives down the far side of a pass to the remote village of Kylerhea, where a summer-only ferry operates to Glenelg.

Opposite the Glen Arroch turning is the only airfield on Skye.

Beyond the crofting township of Breakish, where the old school is the printing works for the *West Highland Free Press* weekly newspaper, the A851 turns off across the moors to the peninsula of Sleat (pronounced Slate) in the south-eastern corner of Skye. The first village is the prosperous and neat-looking Isleornsay, sharing its name with a tidal island which, like the one off Kyleakin, was once owned by Gavin Maxwell. In 1983 part of the island was given over to the commercial growing of a most unusual crop for the Highlands – asparagus.

Beyond Isleornsay the A851 continues to Ostaig, where a Gaelic college has been established, and then to Armadale, the port for the Mallaig car-ferry service. On this section of the Sleat peninsula is the impressive 17,000-acre MacDonald estate. Armadale Castle, set in 40 acres of woodland gardens and nature trails, is the Clan Donald Centre and museum.

Back on the A850 Kyleakin-Portree road, the village of Broadford is built around a sweeping bay. It is the main holiday centre in the southern part of Skye, well placed for sailing, fishing and hill-walking. The A881 turns inland, up the course of the Broadford River, by the marble quarry at Torrin on Loch Slapin, to the end of the road at Elgol.

From this hilltop village there is an

Life Today on Skye

Agriculture is the most important industry in Skye. There are over 1800 crofts on the island but very few are able to support the families that own them and they are usually run as a sideline to supplement the income from other jobs. No-one lives far from the sea and a lot of islanders have small boats for fishing. They put down pots to catch lobsters and crabs which they sell locally or send across to the mainland.

The small clusters of houses scattered over the island are called townships. In the little townships on the north-west, someone like the local postman could well have a croft of 20 acres with two cows and two hundred sheep which also graze the common land. Crofters and their dogs know every sheep in their flock and can tell them apart from the thousands of others which roam the glen. The crofting year starts at the end of November, following the natural cycle of the sheep.

Unless crofters offer bed and breakfast their lives are largely unaffected by the considerable numbers of tourists who visit Skye each year. Tourism is one of the largest industries and in the height of the season, visitors can outnumber the resident population which has fallen to about 6000. In 1840, 23,000 people lived on Skye but lack of work forced them to emigrate to Australia, New Zealand and America. Now, many MacDonalds, MacLeods, MacKenzies and Macphersons return as tourists from these countries 'over the sea to Skye' looking for their roots.

An increasing number of settlers coming to the island are English, drawn by the calm lifestyle and magnificent scenery. They bring skills or offer special services like study holidays for amateur naturalists and organised climbing in the Cuillins. Craftsmen make handicrafts of every variety selling them from small studios attached to their workshops.

Winters can be hard and very windy in the remoter areas. A storm may cut off electricity for several days so households have to be self-sufficient, but the peace and the beauty of the snow-clad hills more than compensate for any inconvenience.

Although most hotels close during the winter, tradesmen, like hairdressers, who cater for the tourists during the season find themselves busy with local trade. Wedding and club dinners normally take place during winter months when residents are able to have the Island and its facilities to themselves.

The sheltered fishing-boat harbour of Portree, the capital of Skye

Dour but ever-popular Dunvegan Castle

Flora MacDonald's grave at Kilmuir

unparalleled view, across Loch Scavaig, to the serrated main ridge of the Cuillin Hills, the finest mountain skyline in Scotland, with a rim of summits over 3000ft. There are cruises from Elgol to the head of Loch Scavaig, where the mountains sweep up directly from the sea.

Returning to Broadford and continuing on the A850 leads through forest plantations, past the sailing centre of Strollamus and the croft-house museum at Luib on the shore of Loch Ainort. The modern main road goes over an inland pass towards the hamlet of Sconser, but the old main road is still open, following the coast.

Sconser starts with Skye's only golf course, a nine-hole layout also grazed by sheep, and an 18th-century inn. On the shore of Loch Sligachan is the slipway for the car and passenger ferry to Raasay, a beautiful island of very pleasant forest, hill and moorland walks. There are many remains of Raasay's contribution to industrial archaeology – an ironstone mine worked from 1913–19, mostly by German prisoners-of-war, for whom the village of Inverarish was originally built.

Back on Skye, beyond the head of Loch Sligachan, with a splendid mountain background, stands the isolated Sligachan Hotel, the major peak of Sgurr nan Gillean rising to the south. This is one of Skye's rock-climbing and hill-walking centres, with trout and salmon in the river nearby.

The A850 goes north of Sligachan by way of Glen Varrigill, where there is a forest walk in the roadside plantations, to Portree, the island's capital. Portree has a fishing-boat harbour at the head of a sheltered bay, a wide selection of hotels and boarding-houses, opportunities for sailing, fishing and walking.

From Portree the A850 cuts diagonally across the island, through Skeabost and Edinbane to the village of Dunvegan. It finishes near Dunvegan Castle, set among woodlands and gardens on one side, on a rock above its sea-loch on the other. This is the most-visited place on Skye, the home for 700 years of the MacLeods of Dunvegan, chiefs of the clan. The castle and its grounds are open on weekdays from Easter to October. And there are boat trips, in season, to the island breeding grounds of the grey seals.

Back at Portree, the main road round the north end of Skye is the A855. It runs along the coast below the mountain ridge of Trotternish, with the isolated rock tower called the Old Man of Storr clearly in view. A forest walk runs through the plantations here.

At Invertote, a minor road turns inland to the abandoned rock workings at Loch Cuithir, alongside the remains of the mineral railway which took supplies to the coast. North of Invertote, a car park and

viewpoint by the edge of a cliff near Elishader look north to the Kilt Rock, given that name because of the basalt columns, rising above the sea, like the pleats of a kilt.

Round the north end of the island, the main road passes close to Duntulm Castle, a ruined clifftop fortress once held by the MacDonald Lords of the Isles. South of Duntulm is the scattered village of Kilmuir. One group of roadside houses has been turned into the Skye Cottage Museum, open on weekdays from May to September.

The most famous place of pilgrimage at Kilmuir is the graveyard on a side-road to the left. Flora MacDonald, the great heroine of the Jacobites, is buried here. In the dark days after the Battle of Culloden in 1746, when Prince Charles Edward Stuart was being hunted by government troops and informers, she smuggled him across from Lewis to Skye, disguised as her maid.

Spread leisurely around a bay, Uig is an important link in the Hebridean ferry services. A car-ferry sails from here to Tarbert in Harris and Lochmaddy in North Uist. Some of the most adventurous motoring in Skye is along a hill road from Uig, across the middle of the Trotternish peninsula towards Staffin, hairpinning down a pass beside the rock of pinnacles of the Quiraing.

Back on the moorlands near Portree, the A856 which leads south from Uig meets up with the A850 Dunvegan road. South of Dunvegan, the B884 wanders into the peninsula between Loch Dunvegan and Loch Bracadale and on to Glendale. This, like so many other districts in Skye, is an area with plenty to visit: an art gallery, a pottery, the Skye Black House Museum, silver and knitwear workshops, and a restored 18th-century water-mill.

In 1904, after leading the movement for land reform, the people of Glendale became the first crofter-landlords in Scotland. The single-track road continues past Waterstein, where a Field Studies Centre offers nature study holidays, to Neist Point. A walk out to the lighthouse is rewarded by panoramic views of the Outer Islands.

Avoiding the turn-off, the recently rebuilt A863 Dunvegan-Sligachan road goes by Bracadale, past the loop-roads to Harlosh and its sub-

aqua diving centre, and to Ullinish. At the head of Loch Harport the B8009 turns off to Carbost and Talisker distillery, the only one on the island.

Off to the left of the B8009, before Carbost, another side-road winds over the moors and through forest plantations to Glenbrittle, the most famous rock-climbing centre on Skye, dominated to the east by the main Cuillin ridge. The highest summit is Sgurr Alasdair, almost 3300ft high. It was first climbed in 1873 by Sheriff Alexander Nicholson. Alasdair is the Gaelic form of Alexander.

The Cuillin ridge is for rock-climbers. It is not at all the place for a casual stroll. But there is a Forestry Commission picnic site by the roadside in the glen, placed so that it offers spectacular mountain views. Lesser mortals can sit quietly there and reflect on the remarkable variety of mountain and coastal scenery on Skye; on its climbing, angling, walking and sailing facilities; on its many craft workshops; on its history and its wildlife – golden eagles, sea-bird colonies, and rare alpine plants growing in remote corries and cliff edges.

Skye has been called the Winged Island, from its shape; the Misty Isle, from its mountain weather; and – as Sheriff Nicolson himself put it – the Queen of all the Isles.

AA recommends:

Hotel: Kinloch Lodge, Isle Ornsay, 1-rosette, 2-star, Country House Hotel, *tel.* 214

Self Catering: Beechwood Holiday Homes, Woodpark, Dunvegan Road, Portree, *tel.* 2634
Cuileag, Isle Ornsay, *tel.* Isle Ornsay 201
Roskhill Barn Flats, Dunvegan, *tel.* 317

Guesthouses: For a selection of guesthouses, please consult the AA guide *Guesthouses, Farmhouses and Inns in Britain.*

Spey Valley

Map Ref: 88NJ0222

Rising unobtrusively in the heights around the Corrieyairack Pass, the Spey is Scotland's second-longest river, almost 100 miles from source to sea. A minor public road follows it down to Laggan Bridge, and by the time it reaches Newtonmore it is ready to flow into the great valley between the Monadliaths and the Cairngorms. This is one of Scotland's busiest holiday areas, winter and summer.

Along this stretch of the Spey Valley, Newtonmore, Kingussie, Kincraig and Aviemore are all bypassed by the latest route of the A9 Perth-Inverness road.

Newtonmore is famous for two sports in particular. This was the first place in the Highlands where pony-trekking was organised; and Newtonmore shinty team, whose field is at the riverside park called the Eilan, is the most successful in the Highlands. The Eilan is where Newtonmore Highland Games are held every August. They feature a rally of Macphersons – this is the heart of the Macpherson country, and the Clan Macpherson Museum, open on weekdays from May to September, is in the village.

By the riverside, Newtonmore also has a pleasant golf course. There is fishing, not just for salmon, brown trout and sea trout in the Spey and in the hill lochs nearby, but also for brown and rainbow trout at Loch Imrich, in the woods in the middle of the village itself.

Beyond Newtonmore is Kingussie, the capital of the district of Badenoch. The Highland Folk Museum, open from April to October, is in six acres of garden ground at the foot of Duke Street. There are indoor and outdoor displays, including a rebuilt Hebridean corn-mill. Footpaths lead

Ice-cold Loch Morlich, Cairngorms

into the birchwoods north of Kingussie, around the hillside golf course, designed by Harry Vardon.

Across the Spey is the ruin of Ruthven Barracks. Now preserved as an Ancient Monument, the barracks were extended from a 14th-century castle, to act as a government stronghold in Jacobite times. It was here, in 1746, that Prince Charles Edward Stuart announced to the remnants of the Jacobite army, ready to fight on after the defeat at Culloden, that the Rising was over.

Back on the north side of the Spey, before the village of Kincraig, but reached from the south by a turn off the A9 at Kingussie, is the Highland Wildlife Park. Open from March to the beginning of November, it was set up to gather together animals and birds which live in the Central Highlands today, and species like wolves and bison, lynx and bear, which have not lived in the wild in Scotland for centuries past. Some of the animals are in enclosures, but others roam free in a 200-acre parkland through which visitors may drive.

Kincraig itself is a smaller place than Kingussie, set among birches

Telford's splendid cast-iron bridge spanning the Spey at Craigellachie

above the Spey and the waters of Loch Inch which, with the marshes alongside, are a world-famous wintering ground for whooper swans from the Arctic. From the Speybank walk there is a splendid view over Inshriach Forest to the Cairngorms.

Loch Inch is the base of a sailing and canoeing school, overlooked by the parish church on a site used for worship since the 7th century. Inside the church is an ancient Celtic church bell. Going beyond the loch, and turning either left or right on to the B970 from Ruthven Barracks, there is a choice of excellent walking country, even without going into the Cairngorms themselves.

Turning right on to the B970 and then taking the minor road up the west side of Glen Feshie leads to a splendid Forestry Commission trail called the Rock Wood Ponds. Towards the end of the public road there is a forest picnic site at Tolvah, looking out over more open ground.

Turning left on to the B970 near Loch Inch leads to Feshiebridge, where there is another picnic site among the pines of Inshirach Forest. A minor road up the east side of Glen Feshie finishes at a nature trail at Achlean, at the very foot of the Cairngorms.

The Speyside Way

Farthest north of Britain's long-distance footpaths, this riverside route starts on the shore of Spey Bay — a fine place for watching gulls and terns, curlews and oystercatchers — at the old Tugnet ice house at the end of the B9104. The ice house is now a museum devoted to Spey salmon fishing.

From Tugnet, the Way follows the east bank of the river, by footpaths and minor roads to Fochabers and Boat o' Brig, passing the Forestry Commission walk and viewpoint beside the weird earth pillars of Aultdearg. More forest tracks and minor roads take it to Craigellachie,

close to one of Scotland's most attractive bridges, the cast-iron single-span with 'chessmen' towers designed by Thomas Telford.

Upstream of Craigellachie, the Way takes to the track-bed of the old Strathspey Railway, which opened in 1863 and closed almost exactly a century later. There is one short stretch of tunnel near Aberlour.

Beyond Aberlour, the old railway crosses to the other bank of the Spey, following a pleasantly wooded and winding course to Ballindalloch. All this is famous angling country, and there are riverside distilleries too; Tamdhu, which was founded in 1897, offers guided tours on weekdays from Easter to September.

Landmark Visitors' Centre, Carrbridge

Strathspey Railway puffs its way from Aviemore to Boat of Garten

Continuing on the B970, past the alpine plant nursery at Inshriach House, another road to the right, about a mile and a half before the junction with the A951 at Inverdruie, goes to a car park and information centre at the Nature Conservancy Council's Loch an Eilein reserve. In the middle of the loch, constantly in view on a rocky island, is the ruin of a 15th-century castle.

Back on the north side of the Spey, Aviemore is the main holiday resort in the district, built up in the late 1960s from a much more modest village. It has a fine array of hotels and chalets, an ice rink, a swimming pool, a shopping centre, fishing on rivers and lochs, a nature trail in the birchwoods immediately behind, and it provides the main accommodation for skiers on the Cairngorm slopes.

The route to the ski slopes is along the A851 past Inverdruie to Coylumbridge, then bearing right on to a road through the pinewoods to Loch Morlich and the Glenmore Forest Park. At more than 1000ft above sea level, Loch Morlich is used for sailing and canoeing, and even has a sandy beach; but it can be cold.

Beyond the loch at Glenmore there is a Forestry Commission information centre, the base for many enjoyable forest and hill walks. Scotland's only commercial reindeer herd is based nearby, and visitors can be taken to see them on their hill grazing. Farther into the glen there is the outdoor centre of Glenmore Lodge. Above the forest line, the 'ski road' swings up to car parks for the ski-tows and chairlifts to the upper slopes.

From Aviemore, the Spey can be

followed by two different routes. The B970 reappears at Coylumbridge and heads along one side of the river towards the turn-off for Boat of Garten. As its name suggests, this village once had a chain-ferry across the Spey, where there is now a road bridge. It has a local museum and a fine golf course. And it is also the end of the volunteer-operated Strathspey Railway, which leaves the British Rail line at Aviemore and runs steam trains through the pinewoods to a temporary terminus at Boat of Garten. There are plans to extend the line on the old track-bed to Grantown-on-Spey.

After the Boat of Garten turn-off, the B970 heads for the village of Nethy Bridge. But a detour on minor roads, through the pines of Abernethy Forest, leads to the RSPB observation centre at the osprey nesting site on the north side of Loch Garten. The ospreys usually arrive in the Highlands in April and leave for Africa in August.

Nethy Bridge is built around a Victorian hotel and the bridge over the River Nethy which gave it its name. Although it was once a timber and iron-working centre, it is now a quiet holiday resort.

From Nethy Bridge the B970 and then the A95 can be followed to Grantown-on-Spey, or a minor road can be taken, across the Spey and so to Grantown by way of Dulnain Bridge. West of Dulnain Bridge, but still considered part of the Spey Valley in holiday terms, is Carrbridge. In the pinewoods south of it is the Landmark Visitor Centre, with displays on the history and wildlife of Strathspey from the ice age to modern times.

Grantown-on-Spey is the most elegant of the resorts in the Spey Valley. It is basically still the planned town of 1766 laid out on the Grant family's estates.

There is an attractive golf course; there are famous fishing beats on the Spey, bowling, tennis and winter curling; the pinewoods between town and river, and on the hills that sweep up behind, provide some of the most beautiful walks in the Highlands. It is a good centre for climbing and skiing. And with all that, Grantown is a place where there is obviously no need to *rush*.

Yachts and windmills on display by a house close to Stonehaven harbour

Among Stonehaven's many festivals and sporting events, the annual RW Thomson Memorial Run for vintage and veteran cars makes the point that the real inventor of the pneumatic tyre – years before Mr Dunlop – was a local man.

A few miles south, on a tremendous clifftop site, the partly-restored Dunnottar Castle is open to visitors. This is where the crown jewels of Scotland were smuggled from during a siege by Cromwell's troops, to be hidden under the floor of the church at Kinneff.

AA recommends:

Garages: Arduthie Motors, Low Wood Road, *tel.* 62989 (day), 64096 (night)
Mitchells, 72 Barclay Street, *tel.* 62077
Moir Motors, Spurryhillock Industrial Estate, *tel.* 64991 (day), 63534 (night)
Stonehaven Motors, 110 Barclay Street, *tel.* 63666
Tough & Johnston, Low Wood Road, *tel.* 62091

Stonehaven

Map Ref: 89NO8685

Recently bypassed by the main Aberdeen road, so that heavy traffic no longer rumbles through the main street of its 18th- and 19th-century town centre, Stonehaven is a well-equipped coastal holiday resort, with sandy beaches along its curving bay.

The fishing town on the south side is built beside a substantial harbour – a good sailing and sea angling base – with a quarter-circle of towering cliffs bending to a rocky point. The restored tolbooth on the way to the harbour now houses a local-history museum.

Strathdon

Map Ref: 89NJ3513

The River Don rises in the lonely hill country beyond the Lecht Road – the A939 from Cock Bridge to Tomintoul, usually the first road in the Highlands to be closed by winter blizzards. Dominating the valley above Cock Bridge is the restored 16th-century Corgaff Castle with its star-shaped ramparts and memories of a violent past. It is open daily from April to September.

Below Corgarff the course of the Don, as it winds through a now-forested valley, is followed by the B973 and then the A97, into the plain east of Kildrummy.

The original Kildrummy Castle was built in the 13th century, and its high-standing ruin, open daily throughout the year, is one of the most complete of its era. The present Kildrummy Castle, now a hotel, was built in 1900. The area from which the stones for it were quarried forms a Japanese water garden and an alpine garden, open from April to October. There is also a small museum.

Bottom: Dunnottar Castle, Stonehaven

Below: Stonehaven harbour, a good base for sailing and sea-angling

Highland Clans

The word 'clan' is from the Gaelic *clann* meaning children and, in a sense, the Highland clansmen were part of individual great families in that they carried the same name, wore the same plaid, lived in the same area and owed loyalty to the same chief. To a large degree territorial boundaries frequently defined the bounds of clanship. For example, the Clan MacNeil territory was enclosed by the sea, and tall mountains were the defence lines of the Macdonalds of Glencoe. Within those boundaries the chief ruled his own clan and looked after their needs; in exchange the clansmen worked for him and fought for him in time of unrest. It was a patriarchal quasi-feudal system which worked well despite occasional internecine feuding. And it was only when 'central government', in the shape of successive Scottish and, latterly, British monarchs, began to intervene and play off one clan against another

that the system eventually began to break down.

In the end it was the relative unity of a large grouping of clans favouring the deposed Stewart dynasty that led to the total destruction of the system when, after the Battle of Culloden in

1746, King George II, with ruthless efficiency, destroyed the power of the chiefs for evermore and, in the process, destroyed much that was finest in Highland culture.

Today some chiefs, like Campbell of Argyll and MacLeod of MacLeod live in their ancestral castles; a few, like the former, live wealthily in their ancestral castles because their forebears had remained loyal to the Hanoverian dynasty and had not risen with Bonnie Prince Charlie in 1745; but they have no powers. Yet, throughout the world, large clan associations maintain the romance of the old tradition and there is still an indefinable sense of kinship among men of the same clan — most emphatically among the emigré communities. There are 84 chiefs on the Standing Council of Clan chiefs which has mild, if not imaginary, discretion over the conduct of clan societies; they represent clans as powerful as the Macdonalds of whom there are hundreds of thousands throughout the world, and the Clan MacThomas of whom the only living male member is the chief — and he is a bachelor.

Farther down the valley of the Don, Alford on the A944 is the site of the Grampian Transport Museum and of a railway museum incorporated in the old main-line station. Both are open from April to September. The station is now the terminus of the narrow-gauge Alford Valley Railway which runs via the Transport Museum into the two country parks of Haughton House and Murray Park, where there are nature trails and picnic sites. The railway operates scheduled services during the months when the museums are open.

Strathpeffer

Map Ref: 84NH4858

This was the most northerly of all Britain's spa resorts, based on the local sulphur and chalybeate springs. Most of the development took place in Victorian times, leaving Strathpeffer with a fine selection of hotels, some having a decidedly Continental look. Although the main spa buildings have gone, the pavilion and the pump room have been preserved. The old railway station has been rebuilt as a centre for craft businesses and an information office.

On the west side, Strathpeffer climbs a ridge with pleasant woodland walks, then dips down again to an energetic golf course. Knock Farril, the corresponding ridge to the east, has more footpaths, including one to an extensive hilltop viewpoint south over the wooded islands of Loch Ussie and north to the 3433ft bulk of Ben Wyvis.

The two-mile stretch of the A832

Tirelessly tumbling Falls of Rogie

north-west of Contin, a short drive from Strathpeffer, leads to Forestry Commission picnic sites in the larch woods by the Blackwater River and among the birches which fringe the beautiful and tranquil Loch Achilty. There are two forest walks from the Blackwater picnic site. Farther upstream, footpaths lead through woodlands to the salmon leap at the Falls of Rogie.

AA recommends:
Hotel: Holly Lodge, 1-rosette, 1-star, *tel.* 21254
Guesthouses: Kilvannie Manor, Fodderty, *tel.* 21389
Beechwood House (farmhouse), Fodderty, *tel.* 21387

The trains are long gone but Strathpeffer station lives on

Strathyre

Map Ref: 91NN5617

Strung along the A84 Callander-Lochearnhead road, Strathyre is a village hemmed in by steep hills and forest plantations. It is in the narrow valley of the River Balvag, which follows a short course from the foot of Loch Voil in Balquhidder, round a ninety-degree turn to the head of Loch Lubnaig, south of the village. When the now-dismantled Callander-Oban railway ran through here, Strathyre was an inland holiday resort, and it is still a centre for hillwalkers and anglers.

At the south end of the village there is a Forestry Commission information centre. A short forest trail goes up the hillside to the east. Across the valley, beyond the Balvag, a much stiffer climb leads to the summit of Ben Shian.

North-west of Strathyre, the Valley of Balquhidder has a minor road along the north side of Loch Voil and Loch Doine. Rob Roy MacGregor is buried in the parish churchyard in Balquhidder village. Beyond Loch Doine, the public road ends at a picnic place at Inverlochlarig, near the site of Rob Roy's house, among the tangle of peaks and mountain passes which he exploited so well in his outlaw days.

AA recommends:
Guesthouse: Rosebank House Hotel, Main Street, *tel.* 208

Right: Ariundle oak reserve

Balquhidder church and ruins of an older church. Rob Roy's grave is here

Strontian

Map Ref: 90NM8161

The crofting estate in the valley of the Strontian River is not owned by a private landlord, but by the government. Strontian village, beside the A861 Ardgour-Salen road, was rebuilt in the 1960s, and has a comprehensive information centre.

The minor road up the glen passes the nature trail through the Ariundle oakwood reserve, which leads towards disused lead mines on the open moorland above. These and other lead mines in the district were worked from 1722 to 1872. Strontium 90, a significant feature of nuclear fallout, takes its name from here.

The hill road, in sight of more deserted lead mines, winds steeply over a pass to a Forestry Commission picnic site with views over Glenhurich Forest and the mountain ridges of Moidart, beyond Loch Shiel. It finishes at the isolated hamlet of Polloch, but the forestry road along the east side of Loch Shiel provides a spectacular walk to Glenfinnan.

AA recommends:
Self Catering: Seaview Grazings Holiday Homes, *tel.* Fort William 2496

Cairngorm Plateau

Nowhere else in Britain is there such an area of ground above 4000ft, alpine or sub-arctic in weather and vegetation, as on the summit level of the Cairngorms, between the Spey Valley and Deeside. The individual mountains — Ben Macdhui, Braeriach, Cairn Toul and Cairn Gorm itself — are not soaring peaks, but the highest points on an undulating plateau dotted with shattered granite tors.

In many places the edge of the plateau is marked by precipices, as cliffs and scree-runs plummet down the corries scooped out by glacier action, often to the chilly waters of a mountain tarn far below.

Almost 100 square miles of the Cairngorms are included in Britain's most extensive National Nature Reserve. Rare birds like the snow bunting and dotterel summer on the plateau itself, while ptarmigan spend the whole year at only slightly lower altitudes.

The easiest way to reach the plateau for a summer walk is by chairlift from the top of the Glenmore ski road. The chairlift takes passengers to the Ptarmigan Observation Restaurant, at 3600ft the highest regularly occupied building in Britain. From here it is just a short walk from the 4084ft summit of Cairn Gorm.

Skiing on the high Cairngorm plateau

Skiing

From a casual turn-of-the-century activity, skiing in the Highlands has developed into an organised sport in four main locations. The busiest area is on the western side of the Cairngorms, where a ski road has been built from Aviemore and Loch Morlich to high-level car parks from which tows and chairlifts operate to the top of the runs in Coire Cas and Coire na Ciste.

The highest main road in Britain — the A93 from Blairgowrie to Braemar — serves the ski centre at Glenshee. In the West Highlands, above the A82 Glencoe road, there are chairlifts and a ski-tow right to the summit of Meall a'Bhuiridh. There is also a skiing centre at the summit of the Lecht Road from Cock Bridge to Tomintoul.

Daily newspapers and radio stations, throughout the season, carry details of the snow conditions at Cairngorm, Glenshee, Glencoe and the Lecht.

All these areas have downhill runs and their own competition programmes. But more and more skiers are tackling cross-country routes, away from the organised centres. One favourite area for this kind of skiing is Glenmore in the western foothills of the Cairngorms.

Tomintoul

Map Ref: 88NJ1618

At 1160ft above sea level, Tomintoul is the highest village in the Highlands, at the northern end of the dramatic Lecht Road which follows the military route of the 1750s between Deeside and Strathspey.

Despite its apparently isolated location among moorlands, farms and forests, Tomintoul is no casually laid-out place. It is to an exact pattern of streets, houses and extensive gardens approved by the Duke of Gordon, who let out parcels of land here in 1776.

The village square fits neatly into this pattern, with solidly built houses, shops and hotels, an information centre and a museum looking over the central green.

South of the village, and most conveniently reached on foot from it, there is a three-mile country walk with fine views of the Avon valley. South-east along the A939 at the Well of the Lecht, a picnic site has been laid out beside a footpath to the site of an 18th-century ironstone mine.

Tomintoul is an angling centre. Trout and salmon permits can be bought in the village, for the fishing beats on the River Avon. The Avon rises high in the Cairngorms and winds down a long and lonely glen to pass west of Tomintoul, continuing south down Strath Avon, where the riverside B9136 is one of many pleasant roads in this often under-rated district.

Tomintoul: the old drinking fountain and village green, and (below) the mainly stone-built village centre

The Trossachs

Map Ref: 91NN5097

The popularity of the Trossachs, over the last 175 years, is due very largely to Sir Walter Scott. He first visited the district in 1790, and used it as the setting for both *The Lady of the Lake*, published in 1810, and for *Rob Roy*, which appeared eight years later. By 1820 the throngs of tourists were so great that the Duke of Montrose, on whose estates many of the places mentioned by Scott were located, had a cattle-drovers' track over the pass from Aberfoyle to Loch Achray rebuilt as a toll-road. The modern A821, opened as a public road only in 1931, uses that same route today.

This is an area of superb natural beauty. Most of it is remarkably unspoiled, thanks to the fact that nearly 70,000 acres are owned by two conservation-conscious organisations – the Forestry Commission and Strathclyde Regional Council Water Department. Both have opened up their 'empires' to provide a great variety of public access and recreation.

From the south, the main-road approach to the Trossachs is by the A81 from Glasgow. As it comes near to Aberfoyle, the A81 runs along the western edge of the flat, reclaimed land of Flanders Moss. The view ahead is totally different – a head-on collision with the Highland Line.

The diagonal ridge of the wooded and craggy Menteith Hills marks the north-east/south-west alignment of the Highland Boundary Fault. On the west side, this range of hills is covered with the spruce plantations of Achray Forest, which stretches westwards across the Duke's Road to Ben Venue. Showing on a minor

hilltop is a radio hut used by the fire-watching service of the Queen Elizabeth Forest Park, which stetches from Achray to Loch Lomond. The lower-lying plantations south and west of Aberfoyle are in Loch Ard Forest.

The A81 itself does not go into Aberfoyle, but turns right along the southern edge of Achray Forest, past Aberfoyle's inevitably hilly golf course and the start of the Forestry Commission's Highland Edge Walk to the hilltop viewpoint of Lime Craig.

Where the A81 turns right, it is the A821 which goes left into the village of Aberfoyle. This is a tourist centre in a magnificent setting, starting at the banks of the infant River Forth and sweeping up the hillside at the first contour lines of the Highlands.

The Bailie Nicol Jarvie Hotel, at the road junction in the centre of the village, takes its name from one of the characters in *Rob Roy*. Immediately south of it, over an old stone-arched bridge, is Kirkton of Aberfoyle, where the ruins of the original parish church recall another literary figure. The Reverend Robert Kirk, parish minister at the end of the 17th century, was an authority on the supernatural. He wrote a very detailed book called *The Secret Commonwealth of Elves, Fauns and Fairies* – and they were firmly believed in the district to have finally carried him away.

Beyond the Kirkton, the public road ends near the manse where Sir Walter Scott stayed while writing about the district. Nearby is the start of the Doon Hill Fairy Trail, mainly for children, with the Reverend Robert Kirk's story in mind.

One waymarked trail farther into Loch Ard Forest leads across the burn which marks the Highland Boundary Fault, passes a wood-ants'

nest and a roe deer clearing, and goes near a long-deserted hamlet on the banks of the sparkling Duchray Water. Lochan Spling, hidden in the forest but easy to reach, is a noted wildfowl site and is also stocked with trout.

West of Aberfoyle, the B829 goes along the foot of steep oak-covered hills to Milton, where there is another forest walk, alongside the tree-fringed Loch Ard with its distant view of Ben Lomond, then on to a junction for Stronachlachar on Loch Katrine and down to Loch Lomondside at Inversnaid.

The most spectacular drive in the Trossachs, and for miles around, is on the A821 as it begins its steep and sharp-cornered climb north from Aberfoyle – the Duke's Road. Off to the right, above the village, is the David Marshall Lodge, a grand viewpoint and the visitor centre for the Queen Elizabeth Forest Park.

Probably the wildest part of the landscape around the Duke's Road is at the old Aberfoyle slate quarries, worked for more than 200 years till 1958. The quarry road survives. Among the deserted workings and spoil heaps there are traces of the quarry village, the smithy, the powder magazine, the mineral railway and the horse tramway which took the finished slates towards the main railway line – also a thing of the past – at Aberfoyle.

Over the summit of the Duke's Road there are the finest views, away into the mountains far to the north. From the Leanach car park, the Wildering forest walks are circular routes in the foothills of Ben Venue. On the north side of the pass, behind Achray Hotel, there is another circular walk into Gleann Riabhach, and that is also the starting point for a hill walk to the 2393ft Ben Venue summit.

Above: Loch Ard in Queen Elizabeth Forest Park, with distant Ben Lomond. Top right: Sir Walter Scott cruising on Loch Katrine. Right: the old Trossachs Church by Loch Achray

Before the top of the Duke's Road, a turning to the right leads into the Achray Forest Drive. Open daily from Easter to September, its seven miles of gravel road pass three lochs, a dozen parking places, information points, a children's play area, viewpoints and picnic sites at places named after the local tree cover, like Larch Point, Pine Ridge and Spruce Glen.

As it comes down off the hills again, the A821 runs along the woodland fringe at the west end of Loch Achray, where there is another parking and picnic area. The loch is used for sailing, water-skiing and angling. On the north side, after the main road turns right at a T-junction, there is a car park near the start of the footpath to the top of Ben A'an. Although the summit is no higher than 1520ft, it is an exposed and genuine peak.

From the junction at the west end of Loch Achray, another road turns left through a little pass to Trossachs Pier in a wooded bay near the foot of Loch Katrine. This is the start of the Water Department estate, which includes the entire catchment area of the loch.

There is plenty of car parking space at Trossachs Pier, beside a tea-room and a fascinating visitor centre, open from May to September, which explains about the expected work of the department, about its fish hatchery, forest plantations, sawmill, sheep and cattle farms. The landward parts of the estate work for their living, too.

Although the public road ends at Trossachs Pier, there are two ways of reaching Stronachlachar at the far end of the loch – and they can be combined, one out and one back. The first is to walk or cycle along the tarmac service road along the north shore, past Glengyle, the birthplace of Rob Roy MacGregor. The other is to sail the eight miles on the department's beautiful Victorian steamer *Sir Walter Scott*, which makes the run from May to September. If its red and white awnings are very turn-of-the-century, it has the modern feature, in a pollution-conscious area, of burning smokeless fuel.

Back at Loch Achray, the A821 continues along the north shore of Loch Venachar, another recreational water, to join the A84 at Kilmahog. A right turn leads to Callander, the town which is the eastern gateway to the Trossachs. It has hotels, boarding houses, shops and tucked-away caravan sites. Permits can be bought for loch and river fishing, and there is an attractive golf course backed by peaceful beechwoods.

North-west, beside the A84 on the way to Strathyre, there are forest walks and a famous salmon leap at the Falls of Leny. A hill road north-east of Callander leads to the Bracklinn Falls. And a strenuous forest walk goes up the steep Callander Crags behind the town. From anywhere on the edge of the cliffs there are magnificent views of the well-conserved hills and forests, lochs and river valleys which make the Trossachs one of Scotland's most beautiful Highland areas.

AA recommends:

Self Catering: Strathyre Forest Cabins, Callander

Guesthouses: Abbotsford Lodge, Stirling Road, Callander, *tel.* 30066

Annfield, 18 North Church Street, Callander, *tel.* 30204

Arden House, Bracklinn Road, Callander, *tel.* 30235

Brook Linn Country House, Leny Feus, Callander, *tel.* 30103

Edina, 111 Main Street, Callander, *tel.* 30004

Greenbank, 143 Main Street, Callander, *tel.* 30296

Highland House Hotel, South Church Street, Callander, *tel.* 30269

Kinnell, 24 Main Street, Callander, *tel.* 30181

Riverview House Private Hotel, Leny Road, Callander, *tel.* 30635

Rock Villa, 1 Bracklinn Road, Callander, *tel.* 30331

The Jacobite Risings

Not all Highlanders were Jacobites, and not all Jacobites were Highlanders — or even Scots. There was a larger interest. The political goal of the Jacobites between 1689 and 1746 was the restoration to the throne of the United Kingdom of the Royal House of Stuart.

Last of the direct line of Stuart kings was James VII of Scotland and II of England, deposed in the Glorious Revolution of 1688. He gave the movement its name — *Jacobus* is the Latin version of James. The Risings of 1708, 1715, 1719 and 1745 were in favour of his exiled son, who was also called James.

But the most charismatic character in the Jacobite story was *his* son Charles Edward Stuart, Bonnie Prince Charlie. That Christian name was no casual diminutive. It is simply the English form of the Gaelic *Tearlaich* or Charles. The defeat of his army at Culloden in 1746 consigned the Stuarts from then on to the footnotes of history.

All the Jacobite Risings were failures in the end. They were mostly financed by France and Spain, making mischief on the greater European scene. But there is still a strong attachment, in many parts of the Highlands, to the memory of those Jacobite days and the romantic figure of Bonnie Prince Charlie, the Young Chevalier.

Ullapool

Map Ref: 84NH1294

Approached by the A835 along the shore of Loch Broom, Ullapool is first seen from the brow of a hill. It is an attractive and unexpectedly sizeable village with a frontage of whitewashed houses and hotels, arranged in regular style on a curve of land which guards its harbour from the open sea. The location and layout were settled by the British Fisheries Society, which founded Ullapool in 1788 as a base for the rich herrings fishings of the Minch.

Ullapool is still an important port. It is the mainland terminal of the car-ferry to Stornoway on the Island of Lewis. And Loch Broom is still busy with fishing boats, whose catches are often bought by foreign factory ships anchored offshore.

However, Ullapool is also a holiday resort. It is a good sailing centre, and there is another one at Altna h-Airbhe on the wild peninsula on the far side of the loch, reached by a weekday ferry which runs from May until September. That ferry link makes it possible to walk over the peninsula to Dundonnell and to Scoraig on Little Loch Broom. Dundonnell House gardens are occasionally open during the summer. And Scoraig is that rarity in modern times, a flourishing village

which has no road connection with the rest of mainland Scotland – and has, indeed, turned down the chance of having one built.

Boat-hirers at Ullapool run cruises to the scattered Summer Isles, home of seals and seabirds. Loch Broom is a noted sea-angling centre. There is also trout and salmon fishing close by, in the River Ullapool and Loch Achall from which it flows.

One of the original buildings set up by the British Fisheries Society, near the harbour, has been turned into the Lochbroom Museum. It was once a fish-curing house, and even now the salt is said to seep from the roof-beams.

North of Ullapool, the A835 continues past the sailing and sea-angling centre at Ardmair Point, looking towards the striking peaks of Coigach. After the bridge over the River Kanaird, a dead-end road to the left leads to Blughasary and the start of a fairly rough-country walk above the Coigach shore.

Northwards again is Drumrunie junction. The main road goes straight ahead here, along the eastern limit of the Inverpolly National Nature Reserve, more than 26,000 acres of mountains, moors and lonely hill lochs. The Nature Conservancy's visitor centre at Knockan Cliff is open from May to September.

Back at Drumrunie, the minor road to the west, leading to Achiltibuie, goes along the shores of Loch Lurgainn and Loch Bad a Ghaill. Angling permits are available at Achiltibuie for these lochs and others actually inside the reserve.

On the north side of Loch Lurgainn is the long ridge of Stac Pollaidh, Scotland's most fantastic collection of rock needles, towers and pinnacles. A footpath from a roadside car park provides a hill-walker's route to that eccentric skyline.

At the far end of Loch Bad a Ghaill, a narrow and twisting road follows the western edge of the Inverpolly reserve to Inverkirkaig

Unloading herring at Ullapool port

Whitehill's sheltered harbour

and Lochinver. Straight on at Badnagyle, minor roads continue to Brae of Achnahaird, Reiff, Alltandhu, Old Dornie, Polbain and, finally, Achiltibuie, the main village in Coigach, strung along the roadside looking out over Badentarbat Bay to the Summer Isles. There is sea-angling and cruising here, and a highly-regarded hotel.

Back at Ullapool, the A835 to the south leads to the forest garden and hillside forest walk at Lael. Where the A835 swings round towards its junction with the A832 from Gairloch, the steep-sided and well-wooded Corrieshalloch Gorge is one of the most dramatic properties of the National Trust for Scotland. Corrieshalloch is a box canyon which provides a spectacular setting for the 150ft Falls of Measach.

One of the best viewpoints, reached by footpaths from both main roads, is a suspension bridge over the gorge. In the midst of all this superb natural scenery there is an unexpected and typically Highland touch. The little bridge was built by Sir John Fowler, co-designer of one of the greatest examples of Victorian engineering – no less a structure than the Forth Bridge.

AA recommends:
Hotels: Ceilidh Place, West Argyle Street, 2-star, *tel*. 2103
Harbour Lights, Garve Road, 2-star, *tel*. 2222
Self Catering: Ardmore, *tel*. 2548 or 2488
Corry Bungalow, *tel*. 2548 or 2488
Corry Hill Bungalow, *tel*. 2548 or 2488
Rhue Baigh Bungalow, *tel*. 2548 or 2488

Whitehills

Map Ref: 89NJ6565

While many fishing villages on the north coast of Grampian base their boats in other harbours, the white-fish fleet here still lands its catches at home, despite the proximity of the much bigger port of Macduff. A fish market bustles into action early every weekday morning, and Whitehills fish are sold, not only in the village itself, but also from vans which have regular runs round towns, farms and villages inland.

There are invigorating walks along the series of bays and headlands which stretch westwards to Portsoy, and a gentler stroll along Boyndie Bay to Banff; but this walk, which passes close to an old chalybeate (mineral water) well favoured by previous generations, also gives an excellent view to the massive cliffs far to the east at Gardenstown and Crovie.

A totally different attraction, 3 miles south-west of Whitehills, is a first-class kart-racing circuit on the former Boyndie airfield.

AA recommends:
Guesthouses: Carmelite House Hotel, Low Street, Banff, *tel*. 2152
Ellerslie, 45 Low Street, Banff, *tel*. 5888

SCOTTISH HIGHLANDS

Atlas

The following pages contain a legend, key map and atlas of the Scottish Highlands, five motor tours and thirteen planned walks in the Highland countryside.

Above: The Queen's View above Loch Tummel

Scottish Highlands Legend

TOURIST INFORMATION (All Scales)

Ⓧ	Camp Site	🦅	Nature reserve
⚘	Caravan Site	☆	Other tourist feature
🅗	Information Centre	🚂	Preserved railway
🅟	Parking Facilities	🐎	Racecourse
🚶	Viewpoint	⚘	Wildlife park
✕	Picnic site	🏛	Museum
▶	Golf course or links	🐾	Nature or forest trail
🏰	Castle	ᛘ	Ancient monument
🕳	Cave	☏ ☏	Telephones : public or motoring organisations
🌿	Country park		
✿	Garden	PC	Public Convenience
🏛	Historic house	▲	Youth Hostel

ORIENTATION

True North

At the centre of the area is 1° 55'E of Grid North

Magnetic North

At the centre of the area is about 6½° W of Grid North in 1986 decreasing by about ½° in three years

GRID REFERENCE SYSTEM

The map references used in this book are based on the Ordnance Survey National Grid, correct to within 1000 metres. They comprise two letters and four figures, and are preceded by the atlas page number.

Thus the reference for **Inverness** appears **88 NH 6645**

88 is the atlas page number

NH identifies the major (100km) grid square concerned (see diag)

6645 locates the lower left-hand corner of the kilometre grid square in which Inverness appears.

Take the first figure of the reference **6**, this refers to the numbered grid running along the bottom of the page. Having found this line, the second figure **6**, tells you the distance to move in tenths to the right of this line. A vertical line through this point is the first half of the reference.

The third figure **4**, refers to the numbered grid lines on the right hand side of the page, finally the fourth figure **5**, indicates the distance to move in tenths above this line. A horizontal line drawn through this point to intersect with the first line gives the precise location of the places in question.

ATLAS 1:500,000 or 8 MILES to 1 INCH

ROAD INFORMATION

M8 ⬡S⬡ 6	Motorway with service area, service area (limited access) and junction with junction number
M9 ⬡L⬡ 5	Motorway junction with limited interchange
M6 ◇ (Mid 1986)	Motorway, service area and junction under construction with proposed opening date
A6 ⬡S⬡	Primary routes } Single and dual carriageway with service area
A516	Main Road }
- - - - -	Main Road under construction
	Narrow Road with passing places
B 6357	Other roads { B roads (majority numbered) / Unclassified (selected)
⊤TOLL	Gradient (1 in 7 and steeper) and toll
▾24 ▾15	Primary routes and main roads
▾24 ▾15	Motorways

Primary Routes

These form a national network of recommended through routes which complement the motorway system. Selected places of major traffic importance are known as Primary Route Destinations and are shown on these maps thus DUNDEE. This relates to the directions on road signs which on Primary Routes have a green background. To travel on a Primary Route, follow the direction to the next Primary Destination shown on the green backed road signs. On these maps Primary Route road numbers and mileages are shown in green.

Motorways

A similar situation occurs with motorway routes where numbers and mileages, shown in blue on these maps correspond to the blue background of motorway road signs.

Mileages are shown on the map between large markers and between small markers in large and small type

1 mile = 1·61 kilometres

GENERAL FEATURES

————	Railway
AA ▪A RAC ▪R PO ▪T	Telephone call box
+-+-+-+-+-+-+-+	National Boundary
- - - - - - - -	County or Region Boundary
🏙 ○	Large Town Town / Village
⊕	Airport
427▪	Height (metres)

WATER FEATURES

 } By Sea { Internal ferry route / External ferry route

Ferry.................. Short ferry routes for vehicles are annotated Ferry

———— Canal

Coastline, river and lake

TOURS 1:250,000 or ¼" to 1 MILE

ROADS   Not necessarily rights of way

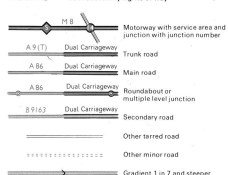

Motorway with service area and junction with junction number

A 9 (T)   Dual Carriageway — Trunk road

A 86   Dual Carriageway — Main road

A 86   Dual Carriageway — Roundabout or multiple level junction

B 9163   Dual Carriageway — Secondary road

Other tarred road

Other minor road

Gradient 1 in 7 and steeper

RAILWAYS

Road crossing under or over standard gauge track

Level crossing

Station

Narrow gauge track

WATER FEATURES

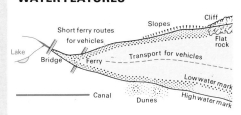

Lake, Bridge, Ferry, Short ferry routes for vehicles, Transport for vehicles, Slopes, Cliff, Flat rock, Low water mark, High water mark, Canal, Dunes

ANTIQUITIES

⁙ Native fortress

------ Roman road (course of)

Castle · Other antiquities

CANOVIVM · Roman antiquity

GENERAL FEATURES

Buildings

Wood

Civil aerodrome (with custom facilities)

Radio or TV mast

Lighthouse

⌒ ⌒ Telephones: public or motoring organisations

RELIEF

Feet	Metres	
		.274 Heights in feet above mean sea level
3000	914	
2000	610	
1400	427	
1000	305	Contours at 200 ft intervals
600	183	
200	61	
0	0	To convert feet to metres multiply by 0.3048

WALKS 1:25,000 or 2½" to 1 MILE

ROADS AND PATHS Not necessarily rights of way

M 8 — Motorway

A 9 (T) — Trunk road

A 86 — Main road

B 862 — Secondary road

Narrow roads with passing places are annotated

A 86 — Dual carriageway

Road generally over 4m wide

Road generally under 4m wide

Other road, drive or track .... Path

RAILWAYS

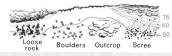

Multiple track   Level crossing

Single track   Cutting

Narrow Gauge

Road over & under   Embankment

Siding   Tunnel

GENERAL FEATURES

♦ Church   with tower
♦ or   with spire   Electricity transmission line
+ Chapel   without tower or spire   pylon pole

Gravel pit

Sand pit

Chalk pit, clay pit or quarry

Refuse or slag heap

NT National Trust always open

NT National Trust opening restricted

FC Forestry Commission pedestrians only (observe local signs)

National Park

HEIGHTS AND ROCK FEATURES

Contours are at various metres / feet vertical intervals

50 ·   Determined   ground survey
285 ·   by   air survey

Surface heights are to the nearest metre / foot above mean sea level. Heights shown close to a triangulation pillar refer to the station height at ground level and not necessarily to the summit.

Vertical Face

75
60
50

Loose rock   Boulders   Outcrop   Scree

RIGHTS OF ACCESS - SCOTLAND

There is no law of trespass in Scotland. However landowners can and do impose restrictions on access such as during the grouse shooting season. They also have a legal remedy against any person causing damage on or to their land and may use reasonable force to remove such a person.

The following simple guidelines should therefore be followed :
Obey restricted access notices and if asked to leave please do so.
Always take care to avoid damage to property and the natural environment.
Common sense, care and courtesy are the watchwords.

The representation on this map of any other road, track or path is no evidence of the existence of a right of access.

WALKS AND TOURS (All Scales)

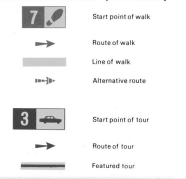

Start point of walk

Route of walk

Line of walk

Alternative route

Start point of tour

Route of tour

Featured tour

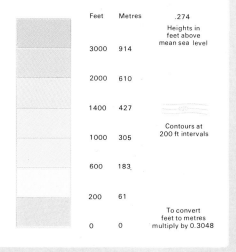

Distances in miles to INVERNESS
Map Ref: 88 NH 6645

SCOTTISH HIGHLANDS

Aberdeen	105	London	569
Dundee	131	Oban	121
Edinburgh	158	Perth	116
Fort William	71	Stirling	150
Glasgow	175	Wick	111

0 Kms	10	20	30	40	50
0 Mls		10		20	30

LEGEND
Motorways	═══════
Primary Roads	───────
'A' Roads	───────
'B' Roads	───────

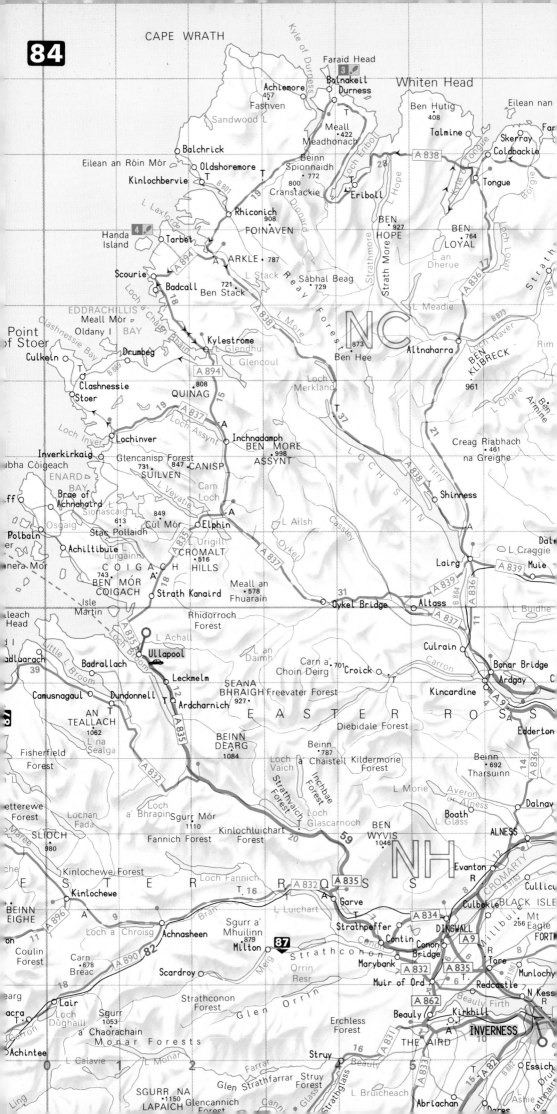

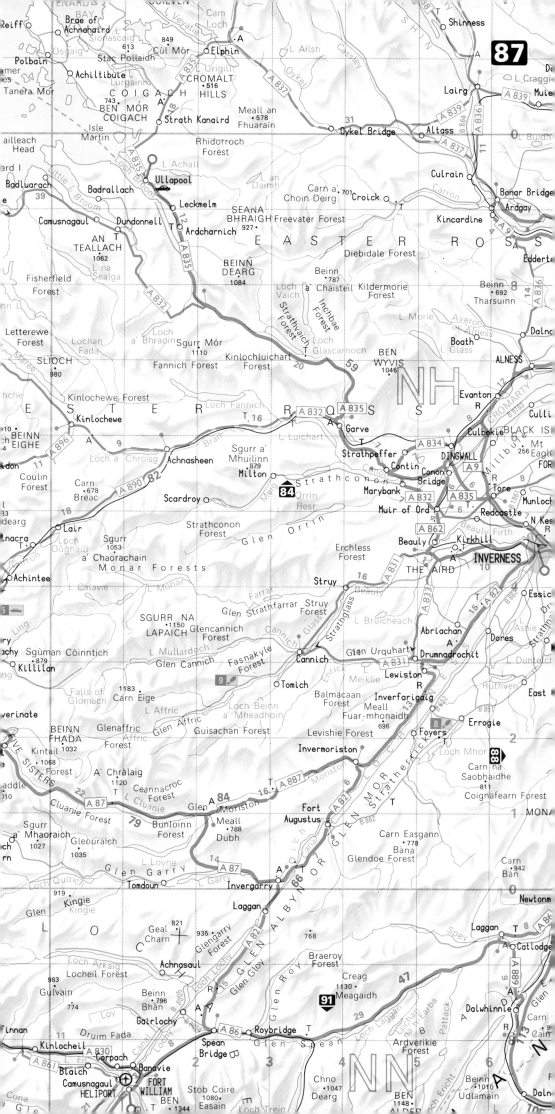

Dalnavie · Kildary · Balintore

Kilmuir · Nigg

INVERGORDON · Nigg Ferry · LOSSIEMOUTH

FIRTH · CROMARTY · BURGHEAD · Hopeman · Duffus · Kingst

Evanton · Balblair · Jemimaville · Burghead Bay · Findhorn · Alves · A 96 · A · ELGIN · Urq

Cullicudden · Kinloss · Garmo

BLACK ISLE · Dyke · FORRES · Rafford · Pluscarden · Longmorn · Lhanbryde

Culbokie · Mt · Rosemarkie · NAIRN · 38 A · Darnaway · Dallas · ROTHES

Eagle · 256 · Forest · B 9010 · Lossie

FORTROSE · Ardersier · Auldearn · A 940 · Archiestown · CHARLE

Tore · Avoch · INVERNESS · Cawdor · Littlemill · OF ABE · DUFFTOWN

Munlochy · Croy · Ferness · Carn · Bellehiglash · BEN RINNES · 841

Redcastle · N Kessock · Balloch · Kitty · Advie

INVERNESS · Daviot · Lochindorb · Carn na Lòine · Tomnavoulin · Corryhabbie Hill · Blackwa Forest

Essich · Drummo · L Moy · GRANTOWN-ON-SPEY · Strath · Knockandhu

Dores · Farr · Carn 659 · Dulnain Bridge · A 938 · Chapeltown · Baden

Ruthven · East Croachy · Carn Glas-choire · Duthil · Nethy Bridge · Tomintoul · Carn Mór · of Gl

Errogie · Tomatin · Carrbridge · Abernethy Forest · LADDER HILLS · Stra

Carn Mhor · Coignafearn · Boat of Garten · Cock Bridge · A 939

Carn na Saobhaidhe · Carn Coire · Geal-charn Mór · Aviemore · Geal Charn 821

Coignafearn Forest · na h-Easgainn · Inverdrule · Loch Morlich · Brown · Cow Hill

MONADHLIATH MOUNTAINS · Alvie · Rothiemurchus · CAIRN GORM · BEN AVON

Kincraig · L Insh · CAIRNGORM MOUNTAINS · BEINN A' BHUIRD

Carn Bàn · KINGUSSIE · Insh · BEN MACDUI 1309 · BEN AVON 1196

Newtonmore · Glen Feshie · Loch Einich · The Devil's Point · Gairn

Laggan · Catlodge · Glenfeshie Forest · FOREST OF MAR · Braemar · A 93 · Balmoral Cas

Dalwhinnie · Carn na Caim · Gaick Forest · Geldie Burn · Inverey · Balmoral Forest

Beinn Udlamain · BEINN DEARG · Tarf Wr · Beinn Iutharn Mhór · The Cairnwell · BROAD CAIRN · LOCHNAGAR

FOREST OF ATHOLL · BEINN A' GHLO · Devil's Elbow · GLAS MAOL · Braedownie · MAYAR

Dalnaspidal · Glen Tilt · Spittal of Glenshee · Auchavan

Loch Errochty · Blair Atholl · BEN VRACKIE · A 924 · Forter · Folda

BEINN A' CHUALLAICH · Killiecrankie · Creag Dhubh · Kirkmichael · Blacklunans · Backwater Resr

Kinloch Rannoch · Tummel Bridge · Queen's View · Moulin · Forest of Alyth · Bridge of Cally

SCHIEHALLION · Foss · PITLOCHRY · Ardle · ALYTH

CARN MAIRG · Meall Tairneachan · Grandtully · Ballinluig · Bridge of Cally · A 94

Keltneyburn · Weem · Balnaguard · Forest of Clunie · RATTRAY

Fortingall · Kenmore · ABERFELDY · Dowally · BLAIRGOWRIE · MEIGLE

BEN LAWERS · Acharn · Garrow · Dunkeld · L of Lowes · COUPAR ANGUS

Lawers · Ardtalnaig · Trochry · Inver · Birnam · A 984 · Caputh · Meikleour · Burrelton

Bridge of Balgie · Amulree · Meall nan Caorach · Bankfoot · Airntully · Cargill · King's Seat

Ardeonaig · BEN CHONZIE · Harrietfield · Stanley · Guildtown · Collace · A 923

Loch Lednock Resr · Glen Almond · Luncarty · A 93 · Balbeggie

A 942 FINDOCHTY PORTKNOCKIE PORTSOY
KINNAIRD HEAD
BAY UCKIE CULLEN Troup Hd ROSEHEARTY Sandhaven FRASERBURGH
Portgordon 61 Whitehills BANFF MACDUFF Pennan Inverallochy St Combs
A 98 Fordyce A 98 Gardenstown New Aberdour Memsie A 981 Rathen
Kirktown of Deskford Kirktown of Alvah Longmanhill A 98 15 A Mormond Hill Crimond New Leeds Rattray Head
abers Cornhill Knock Hill 430 B 9105 New Byth New Pitsligo Strichen A 92 18
Newmill KEITH Knock ABERCHIRDER TURRIFF Cuminestown Fetterangus Rora Loch of Strathbeg
A 96 Milltown Inverkeithny Deer's Hill 178 New Deer Maud Mintlaw Longside PETERHEAD
NJ STRATHBOGIE Ythanwells Kirktown of Auchterless Fyvie Methlick Stuartfield Old Deer Clola Burnhaven Boddam Buch Ness
HUNTLY Rothienorman A 947 Ythanbank Auchnagatt Hill of Dudwick Hatton A 952 Cruden B
Tap o' Noth 564 Kirkton of Culsalmond Insch A 920 Meikle Wartle Tarves FORMARTINE ELLON Collieston Bay o Crude
A 941 Rhynie Kennethmont Kirkton of Rayne OLDMELDRUM Pitmedden Newburgh A 975 LERWICK (14 hrs)
BUCK 721 Lumsden Clatt 487 Leslie Oyne GARIOCH Udny Green Foveran
CORREEN HILLS Tullynessle Auchleven 528 BENNACHIE INVERURIE Newmachar Balmedie
Kildrummy Keig KINTORE Hatton of Fintray Belhelvie
Towie Alford Monymusk Kemnay Blackburn Dyce A 92 Bridge of Don
Craigievar Castle Sauchen A 96 Stoneywood Stoneywood
Migvie A 944 Dunecht L of Skene Bucksburn ABERDEEN Girdle Ness
Tarland Lumphanan HILL OF ECHT Cults A 93 A 956
CROMAR Ordie MAR FARE 471 Peterculter Cove Bay
57 Torphins 14 A 93 Crathes Castle A Dee Portlethen Downies
Dinnet Aboyne Kincardine A. O'Neil BANCHORY Kirkton of Durris Newtonhill
Forest of Marywell A 980 Strachan A 957 Muchalls
BALLATER Glen Tanar Forest Peter Hill 617 Kerloch 534 Cowie Wr STONEHAVEN
Mount Keen 939 Mount Battock Drumlithie A 94 Bruxie Hill
L Lee Tarfside NO Glen T Esk Auchenblae Roadside of Kinneff Catterline
778 White Hill HOWE OF THE MEARNS Arbuthnott Kinneff
Fettercairn INVERBERVIE
Bridgend Edzell LAURENCEKIRK Gourdon 71
Kirkton of Menmuir Inchbare 93 Luthermuir Marykirk St Cyrus Johnshaven Milton Ness
Fern Hillside A 937
Cortachy Tannadice A 94 BRECHIN A 935 MONTROSE Scurdie Ness
KIRRIEMUIR Oathlaw Bridge of Dun Farnell Ferryden
FORFAR Aberlemno Guthrie Friockheim Lunan Bay Inverkeilor
Glamis A 929 Inverarity Letham St Vigeans
Cormyllie ARBROATH
gray A 929 Monikie Muirdrum Arbirlot
4 Newbigging Barry East Haven
CARNOUSTIE
TOLL MONIFIETH A 930 Broughty Ferry Buddon Ness

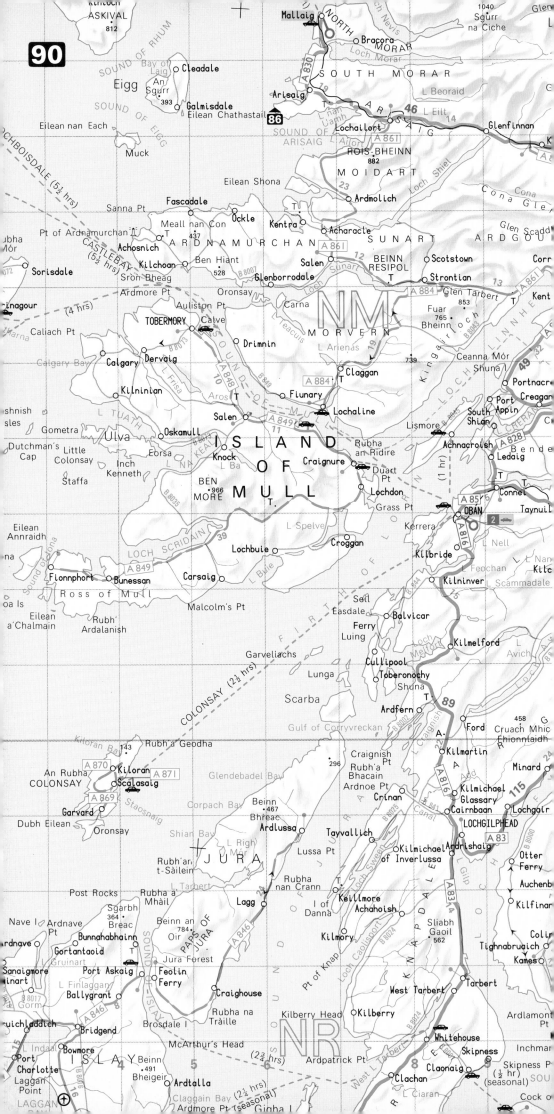

TOUR 1
Lochs, Forests and Falls

Starting with views of Gairloch's sandy bays and the island-studded expanse of Loch Maree, the drive follows the rivers and skirts the lochs of this gentle corner of Wester Ross, passing the beautiful Falls of Measach and the lush vegetation of Inverewe Gardens on its way.

The drive starts from Gairloch, a village with a fine, sandy beach occupying an attractive position on the shore of Loch Gairloch. A converted farmhouse contains the Gairloch Heritage Museum which depicts life in the area from prehistoric times to the present day.

Leave by the A832 Kinlochewe road. After passing through Charlestown the road proceeds inland, following the course of the River Kerry, and becomes single track before reaching the Gairloch Dam. The drive continues into the Slattadale Forest, with the Victoria Falls on the right, to the edge of Loch Maree which has many small, tree-clad islands scattered over it. Across the water the mountain peaks of Letterewe Forest can be seen, with Slioch (3215 ft) rising prominently. The road widens as it runs alongside the loch, skirting the Beinn Eighe Nature Reserve on the approach to Kinlochewe. Several nature trails and a Visitor Centre have been provided in the Reserve.

Gairloch's beautiful sands offer views of the Torridon Hills

Corrieshalloch Gorge has spectacular falls

At Kinlochewe keep on the A832 (single track) Achnasheen road. The drive climbs through Glen Docherty and later skirts Loch a' Chroisg before arriving at the hamlet of Achnasheen. Continue forward, signed Inverness, along Strath Bran – with Loch Luichart on the right – as you approach Gorstan.

At Gorstan turn left on to the A835, signed Ullapool. From here the drive follows the Black Water, then the Glascarnoch River, before passing the Loch Glascarnoch Reservoir on the right. Beyond the loch, bleak Dirrie More is crossed before reaching the Braemore road junction.

Turn left here on to the A832 where there is a carpark for the Corrieshalloch Gorge (NTS). The Gorge and the spectacular Falls of Measach can be viewed from a suspension bridge which spans the deep and narrow chasm. The A832 climbs on to higher ground before descending to the Dundonnel River beneath the slopes of An Teallach (3484 ft). From Dundonnel the tour follows the shoreline of Little Loch Broom, passing Ardessie where there is a fish farm which is open to the public. Later the road crosses a headland and rejoins the coast at Gruinard Bay – noted for its sandy beaches. Gruinard Island in the middle of the bay was used as a germ warfare-testing ground in World War II; it is still infected with anthrax and landing is prohibited. At the small hamlet of Laide the road swings southwards to the outskirts of Aultbea – a small crofting village situated on Loch Ewe.

Continue along the coast road. After 6 miles, on the right, is the entrance to Inverewe Gardens (NTS). These, begun in 1862, contain a remarkable collection of rar" and sub-tropical plants. At Poolewe the road turns southwards again and in one mile there is a viewpoint from where the length of Loch Maree can be seen. Higher ground and somewhat barren countryside is traversed before the return to Gairloch.

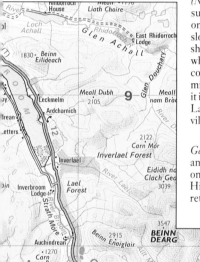

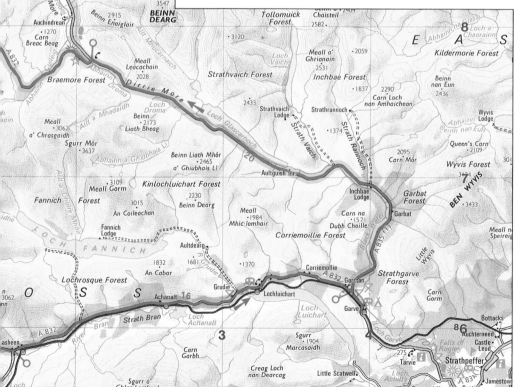

TOUR 2 102 MILES
Castles, Crags and Moorland

Leaving the bustling town of Oban, the tour climbs up to the forbidding Pass of Brander, crosses desolate Rannoch Moor, then goes through historic Glen Coe, before returning to the less dramatic scenery – scattered with castle ruins – of Loch Linnhe.

The drive starts from Oban, a popular resort and the port serving the islands of Mull, Coll, Tiree, Lismore, Colonsay, Barra and South Uist. Of interest around the town are McCaig's Folly (the famous circular landmark above the harbour built to relieve unemployment in the late 19th century), the Caithness Glassworks, Macdonald's Mill, which demonstrates spinning and weaving, and, a mile to the north-west, the ruins of 13th-century Dunollie Castle.

Follow signs Crianlarich to leave by the A85. After 3 miles the road to the left leads to ruined 13th-century Dunstaffnage Castle (AM) which stands at the mouth of Loch Etive. Later, on the approach to Connel, the Falls of Lora can be seen below Connel Bridge. Continue beside the loch to Taynuilt. (A 1½-mile detour may be taken from here to the 18th-century Bonawe Iron Furnace (AM). At the crossroads turn left on to the B845, signed Village, and in ½ mile turn right, unclassified). Beyond Taynuilt, twin-peaked Ben Cruachan (3695 ft) rises to the left of the road. The main drive enters the wild Pass of Brander and later, on the left, are the Falls of Cruachan below the Cruachan Reservoir. The power station and Visitor Centre opposite are built underground. The road continues alongside Loch Awe and after 2¾ miles is the attractive church of St Conan, built between 1881 and 1930. Later, beyond Lochawe Post Office, there are views of the ruins of Kilchurn Castle (AM).

Pass Dalmally then 2 miles farther turn left on to the B8074, signed Glen Orchy. The single-track road passes through partly forested valley scenery featuring several waterfalls. (An easier, alternative route to Bridge of Orchy is via the A85 to Tyndrum, then left on to the A82; it is 5 miles longer.)

After 10¼ miles on the B8074 turn left on to the A82, signed Fort William, and continue to Bridge of Orchy. Beyond the village the road passes Loch Tulla then climbs on to the bleak bog and lochan waste of Rannoch Moor. The Kings House Hotel, on the right, faces Stob Dearg (3345 ft), one of Scotland's most famous rock peaks, which lies in a well-known winter sports district. From here the road descends into rugged Glen Coe, overshadowed by the peaks of Bidean nam Bian, at 3766 ft the highest mountain in Argyll, and its outliers, the Three Sisters. One mile beyond Loch Achtriochtan on the right is the Glen Coe Visitor Centre (NTS). This stands ½ mile from Signal Rock, from which the signal was given for the hideous massacre of the Macdonalds of Glencoe by the Campbells of Glen Lyon in 1692. Continue down the glen to Glencoe village. Two heather-thatched cottages in the main street house the Glencoe and North Lorn Folk Museum, with Macdonald and Jacobite relics.

From Glencoe follow signs Oban and Fort William and at the roundabout, 1¾ miles past the edge of Ballachulish, take the second exit A828, signed Oban. Shortly the road runs beneath the impressive Ballachulish Bridge then past the Ballachulish Hotel. Nearby is a monument to James of the Glen, wrongly hanged in 1752 after a notorious trial known as the Appin murder case. The drive then follows the Appin shore of Loch Linnhe, through Kentallen and Duror, with views of the Ardgour Hills across the loch. Early 16th-century Castle Stalker can be seen near Portnacroish, before the drive meets the edge of Loch Creran. It continues round the loch to the Sea Life Centre and Marine Aquarium at Barcaldine, with several picnic sites and forest walks along the way. Later there are views of Barcaldine Castle to the right. Continue through Benderloch, skirting Ardmucknish Bay; from here, the Moss of Achnacree can be seen over to the left.

After 2¼ miles go under a railway bridge and bear right to cross the cantilevered Connel-bridge. At the T-junction turn left on to the A85 for the return to Oban.

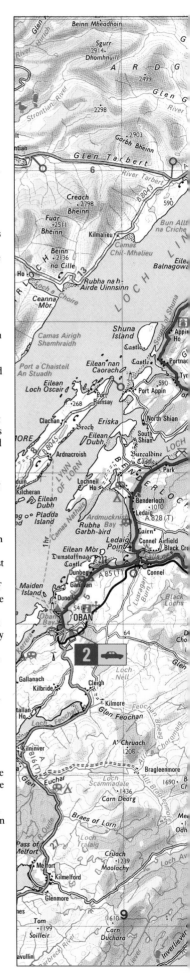

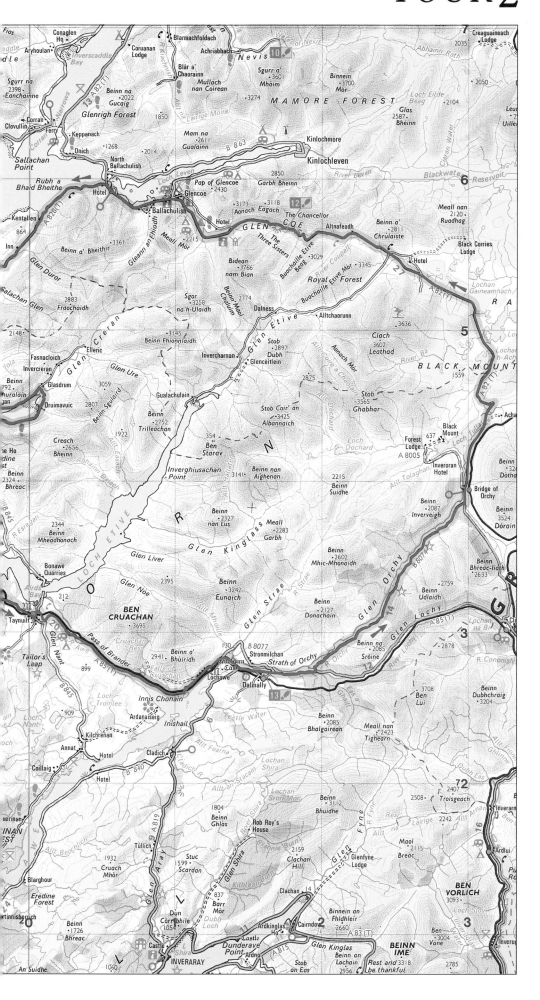

TOUR 3 98 MILES
Mountain, Woodland and Water

The mountainous area known as Breadalbane is visited on the early part of this tour, followed by a fine run along the entire western shoreline of Loch Lomond. The final part is through the Trossachs with unparalleled landscapes of mountains, lochs, rivers and woodland.

The drive starts from Callander, an attractive resort and touring centre.

Follow signs Crianlarich to leave by the A84. After the hamlet of Kilmahog, complete with woollen mill, the tour passes through the Pass of Leny, in which the Falls of Leny can be seen to the left. The wooded eastern shore of Loch Lubnaig is then followed to reach the village of Strathyre, where the Strathyre Forest Centre is located. Two miles farther, at the Kingshouse Hotel, pass the turning to Balquhidder. Rob Roy is buried in the churchyard of the roofless Balquhidder Kirk. The tour continues northwards.

At the small inland resort of Lochearnhead keep forward on to the A85, still signed Crianlarich, entering the gloomy gorge of Glen Ogle before turning westwards to follow the River Dochart through Glen Dochart. The Breadalbane Hills lie to the right and later the peak of Ben More (3852ft) is seen to the left. The tour then runs alongside Loch Iubhair and Loch Dochart to reach Crianlarich.

At Crianlarich turn left on to the A82, signed Glasgow. Picturesque Glen Falloch is then entered and after 4½ miles the road passes the Falls of Falloch (on left). Continuing through the hamlet of Inverarnan, the drive soon reaches Ardlui – situated at the head of Loch Lomond, the largest loch in Scotland. A magnificent 20-mile run is then made along its entire western shoreline.

Continue with the A82, still signed Glasgow. A further 8 miles on there is the picturesque village of Luss, another calling point for the Loch Lomond steamers. Television viewers may recognise the location as being 'Glendarroch' from the series *Take the High Road.* The widest part of Loch Lomond is seen beyond Luss. Later the A82 veers away from the shoreline, but returns again to reach the Duck Bay picnic area.

Pass Duck Bay and in 1¾ miles, at the roundabout, take the first exit on to the A811 (signed Stirling) to reach the outskirts of Balloch. Situated at the southern end of Loch Lomond, Balloch is the starting point for steamers.

At the roundabout take the second exit. (For Balloch and Cameron Park take first exit). At the next roundabout, again take the second exit and shortly pass the turning for Balloch Castle Country Park. Contained within the 200 acres of parkland beside Loch Lomond is the 19th-century Balloch Castle, which is open to the public.

Continue on the A811 to Gartocharn, then in 3¼ miles at the T-junction turn left. Four miles farther bear left to join the A81, signed Aberfoyle. In 6¼ miles bear left again on to the A821 and enter Aberfoyle. Situated in the upper Forth valley, the small resort of Aberfoyle is known as the 'Gateway to the Trossachs' and has associations with Sir Walter Scott's *Rob Roy.* Loch Ard Forest to the south and Achray Forest to the north form the Queen Elizabeth Forest Park.

In Aberfoyle, at the Bailie Nicol Jarvie Hotel, turn right (signed the Trossachs and Callander). An ascent is then made to follow a fine touring route known as the 'Duke's Road'. It was built by the Duke of Montrose in the 19th century. Shortly, pass the entrance to David Marshall Lodge – a Forest Park Visitor Centre which includes an AA viewpoint. The winding Duke's Pass is followed through the Achray Forest and after 1¾ miles the tour passes the entrance to the Achray Forest Drive. After another mile their is a hilltop viewpoint.

In another 2 miles turn left for Loch Katrine. Loch Katrine, which inspired Scott's poem *The Lady of the Lake,* is set in the heart of the Trossachs, with Ben Venue (2393ft) prominent to the south. Pleasure boat trips operate from the pier at the eastern end of the loch.

Return along the same road, then keep forward with the A821, signed Callander (A84). After Brig o'Turk the road runs alongside Loch Venachar, with the 2882ft peak of Ben Ledi to the left. *Later cross the River Leny and turn right on to the A84 to return to Callander.*

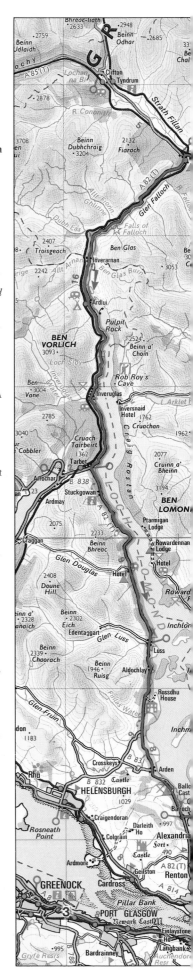

Loch Katrine inspired Sir Walter Scott: his name adorns a steamer on the lake

Kirk at Loch Achray, silhouetted against the Trossachs sky

Loch Lomond from the A82: a magnificent 20-mile route

TOUR 4 94 MILES
Ski slopes, Reindeer and Whisky

From Aviemore, the heart of Britain's finest winter sports district, the tour makes its way through dense forests and beautiful mountain scenery, passing many interesting places, including the Highland Wildlife Park, the Glenlivet Distillery and the Landmark Centre.

The drive starts from Aviemore, one of Scotland's major inland resorts since the Aviemore Centre, a massive complex of entertainment and sporting facilities, was built in the 1960s.

Leave by the B9152 Perth road. After 2½ miles a monument to the Duke of Gordon can be seen to the left, with Loch Alvie on the right. Beyond the village of Kincraig is the Highland Wildlife Park where there are many species of animals native to Scotland, past and present, including wolves and bears.

In 3¼ miles go forward on to the A86, signed Kingussie and Fort William, to enter Kingussie. This is the largest town in upper Strath Spey and has an interesting Highland Folk Museum with a reconstructed Hebridean mill and a primitive 'black house'.

Turn left on to the B970, singed Ruthven and Insh. (For a detour to Newtonmore, where there is the Clan Macpherson House and Museum containing relics of the clans and Prince Charles Edward Stuart, keep foward along the A86 for 3 miles.) The tour continues across the valley and underneath the A9, then bears left and passes the remains of Ruthven Barracks, built in 1716 and added to later by General Wade, the famous Highland road-maker.

In another 1¾ miles cross the River Tromie and turn left, signed Kincraig. Continuing through the hamlet of Insh, in 2¾ miles the drive keeps forward with the Rothiemurchus road and later crosses the River Feshie at Feshiebridge. Beyond this hamlet the drive enters the attractive Inshriach Forest and after ¼ mile a road on the right leads to the Feshiebridge Picnic Area. (After 4½ miles a short detour can be made by turning right on to an unclassified road to visit the shores of Loch an Eilein. The ruined island castle here – not open – was a stronghold of the notorious Wolf of Badenoch, outlawed son of Robert II, Scotland's first Stuart king).

Continue with the B970 to Inverdruie, then turn right, signed Coylumbridge. Immediately pass the Cairngorm Visitor and Whisky Centre then continue to Coylumbridge, a small village on the River Druie. (The unclassified road ahead, signed Glenmore, leads into the Cairngorm Mountains, passing through the Queen's Forest and beside Loch Morlich. This ski road climbs to nearly 2250 ft and the main chairlift is open all year. The whole area is now part of Glen More Forest Park and reindeer were introduced here in 1952. The Cairngorms form a vast National Nature Reserve covering some 60,000 acres. This diversion is 15 miles long.)

From Coylumbridge turn left with the B970, signed Nethy Bridge, and continue along Strath Spey. In 7 miles turn right on to an unclassified road, signed Loch Garten, to enter Abernethy Forest and after 1½ miles pass Loch Garten. Half a mile beyond the loch keep forward on to the Nethy Bridge road and in 2¼ miles turn right, signed Grantown-on-Spey, to rejoin the B970 for Nethy Bridge, a small resort on the Rivery Nethy. After crossing the river turn right (no sign) and in ½ mile go over the crossroads, signed Dorback and Tomintoul. After 4½ miles turn right on to the A939 towards Tomintoul. The Hills of Cromdale rise away to the left while the Cairngorms are prominent to the right. Climbing first to a height of 1500 ft, the drive then descends to the Bridge of Brown and then ascends and descends again before crossing the Bridge of Avon.

Turn left here on to the B9136, signed Craigellachie. The tour follows the prettily wooded Strath Avon and after 7½ miles passes the Drumin Picnic Site. In another 1¾ miles a road on the right leads to the Glenlivet Distillery.

Continue over the River Livet and turn left on to the B9008, signed Whisky Trail. Four miles along the valley, at the Dalnashaugh Inn, turn left on to the A95 Grantown road and recross the River Avon to enter Strath Spey. Continue through the hamlet of Cromdale before reaching Grantown-on-Spey, beautifully situated amid woods and mountains.

Leave Grantown by the A95 Perth road and at Dulnain Bridge keep forward on to the A938, signed Carrbridge. After 6¾ miles turn left on to the B9153, signed Aviemore, to enter Carrbridge. This small village has developed rapidly as a winter sports centre and summer resort. Attractions at the Landmark Centre include a sound and vision presentation of Highland history.

Continue for 2½ miles then go forward on to the A95. In another 2½ miles go forward again on to the B9152 to return to Aviemore.

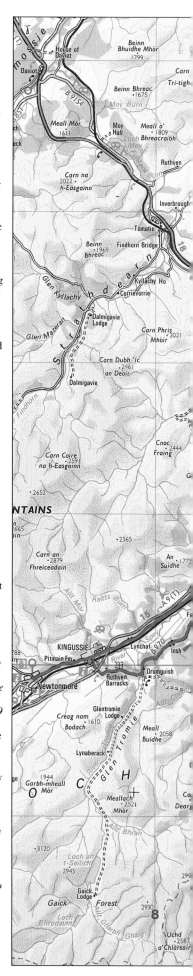

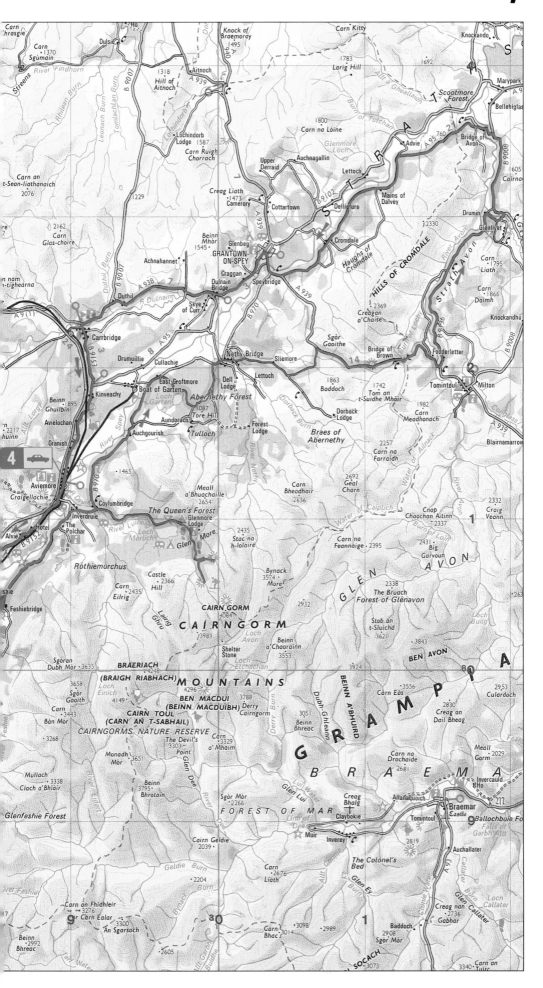

Carn
Chrasgie
Ho
Streens

Carn · 1370
Sgùmain
Dulsie

River Findhorn
Leonach Burn
Rhitean Burn
B 9007
Tomlachlan Burn

Carn an
t-Sean-liathanaich
2076

Carn an
t-Sean-liathanaich
2076

Carn Glas-choire
2162

7

n nam
n-tighearna

A9(T)

Carrbridge

B 9153

Drumuillie

Beinn
Ghuilbin
1895

Kinveachy

Avielochan

Granish

4

Aviemore
Craigellachie

Inverdruie
The
Polchar
Alvie

B 9152

Feshiebridge

Rothiemurchus

1465

Coylumbridge

The Queen's Forest

River Spey
B 970

Knock of
Braemoray
1495
940

Carn Kitty

Knockando

Aitnoch
A 939
Hill of
Aitnoch
1318

Lochindorb
Lodge 1587

Carn Ruigh
Chorrach

Creag Liath
· 1473
Camerory

Cottartown

Upper
Derraid

Knock of
Braemoray

A 939

Beinn
Mhòr
1545

Glenbeg

GRANTOWN-
ON-SPEY

Craggan

Dulnain
Bridge

Duthil

Skye
of Curr

Nethy Bridge

Cullachie

East Groftmore

Dell
Lodge

Lettoch

Boat of Garten

Loch
Garten

Abernethy Forest

1087
Tore Hill

Aundorach

Auchgourish

Tulloch

Meall
a'Bhuachaille
2654

Glenmore
Lodge

Glen More

Stac na
h-Iolaire
2435

Carn
Eilrig
2435

Castle
Hill
· 2366

Sgòran
Dubh Mòr · 3635

Sgòr
Gaoith
3658

Carn
Bàn Mòr · 3443
4149

· 3268

Mullach
Clach a'Bhlàir
3338

Beinn
Bhrotain
3795·

Glenfeshie Forest

Monadh
Mòr
3651

Carn an Fhidhleir
· 3276
9r Carn Ealar

Beinn
Bhreac
2992

3300
An Sgarsoch

· 2605

iver Feshie

LÀRIG
GHRU

Loch
Morlich

Lagg Dhubh

CAIRN GORM
4084

CAIRNGORM
3983

BRAERIACH
4248
(BRAIGH RIABHACH)

Loch
Einich
4296

BEN MACDUI
3788
(BEINN MACDUIBH)

CAIRN TOUL
(CARN AN T-SABHAIL)

CAIRNGORMS NATURE RESERVE
The Devil's
Point
3303

Derry
Cairngorm

Carn
a'Mhaim
3329

Sgòr Mòr
·2266

Cairn Geldie
2039·

2204

Carn
·2676
Liath

Geldie Burn

Bynack
Burn

Carn
Bhac
3014

MOUNTAINS

Shelter
Stone

Loch
Etchachan

Beinn
a'Chaorainn
3553

Loch
Avon

2932

Bynack
More
3574·

Carn na
Feannaige · 2395

1783
Larig Hill

1692

A 95 760

Advie

Scootmore
Forest

Bridge of
Avon

B 9008

Marypark

A 9

Belleheiglash

1800
Carn na Lòine

Glenmore
Loch

Auchnagallin

Lettoch

Mains of
Dalvey

Delliefure

Cromdale

HILLS OF CROMDALE

Creagan
a'Chaise
· 2369

Haughs of
Cromdale

1863
Baddoch

Sgòr
Gaoithe

Sliemore

Dorback
Lodge

Braes of
Abernethy

Forest
Lodge

1982
Carn
Meadhonach

Carn na
Farraidh
2257

Carn
Bheadhair
2636

Geal
Charn
2692

Cnap
Chaochan Aitinn
· 2337

Carn na
Drochaide
2681

Carn na
Feannaige

Stob an
t-Sluichd
3621

The Bruach
Forest of Glenavon
2338

BEN AVON
3843

GLEN AVON

Big
Garvoun
2431

2330

Glenlivet

Carn
· 1795
Liath

Carn
· 1866
Daimh

Knockandhu

Fodderletter

Tomintoul
14
Milton

Bridge of
Brown

Burn of Tulchan

Strath Avon

River Avon

Water of Ailnack

Burn of Loin

Blairnamarrow

A 939

Conglass

2332
Craig
Veann

· 263

Loch
Builg

1

3556
Càrn Eàs

2953
Culardoch

2830
Creag an
Dail Bheag

Meall
Gorm
2029

80

GRAMPIAN

BRAEMAR

Invercauld
Ho

Braemar
Castle

Ballochbuie Fo

Falls of
Garbh Allt

Auchallater

Creag nan
2736
Gabhar

Loch
Callater

Glen Callater

Carn an
Tuirc

Allt an t-Slugain

BEINN A'BHUIRD
3924

Dubh Ghleann

3051
Beinn
Bhreac

FOREST OF MAR

Glen Lui

Lui Water

Creag
Bhalg

Allanaquoich

Tomintoul

Claybokie

Muir

Inverey

The Colonel's
Bed

2819

Derry Burn

River Dee

Glen Dee

Sgòr Mòr
·2266

Glen Ey

Allt Connie

3098
2989
3014

Baddoch
2908
Sgòr Mòr

3073
SOCACH

1

3340

River Garry

TOUR 5

Crofts, Isles and Wildlife

This tour hugs the coastline of the Applecross Peninsula, encompassing wide, open views and passing through tiny, remote hamlets, before entering the splendid Glen Torridon – famous for its wealth of wildlife – then meandering along the course of the River Carron.

The drive starts from Lochcarron, and attractive village standing on the shore on Inner Loch Carron. An unclassified road to the south-west leads past the small fishing harbour at Slumbay to Stromemore, where there is ruined Strome Castle (NTS).

Leave by the A896 Shieldaig road. The single-track road leads on to high ground then descends to Kishorn post office on Loch Kishorn. Across the water a fabrication yard for the North Sea oil industry can be seen.

Continue alongside the loch for 1½ miles and turn left on to an unclassified road, signed Applecross. (Alternatively, keep forward with the A896 and begin the directions again at Shieldaig: this saves nearly 28 miles.) The main drive starts to climb the spectacular Bealach na Ba (Pass of the Cattle), following a narrow, winding road with hairpin bends. The maximum gradient is 1 in 5 and the summit at 2053 ft makes it one of the highest roads in Britain. An AA viewpoint here offers wide views over the Inner Sound to the Isle of Skye. A long, but less difficult, descent is made across rugged terrain to the isolated village of Applecross.

Leave by the Shieldaig road and continue round Applecross Bay. A scenic run is then made along the Inner Sound through remote country with good views towards the islands of Skye, Raasay and Rona. After passing the few cottages at Fearnmore, the drive turns south-eastwards beside Loch Torridon. Beyond the turning for Kenmore the road becomes narrower and more winding as it follows the shore to Loch Shieldaig.

At the junction with A896 turn left to reach Shieldaig. This small crofting village stands on the edge of the loch of the same name. The double-track Torridon road rounds the southern shoreline of Upper Loch Torridon, offering magnificent views across the water to the Torridon Mountains – including Beinn Alligin rising to 3232 ft. Later the drive passes through Annat to reach the turning for Torridon village. To the left is the National Trust for Scotland Countryside Centre which has audio-visual equipment giving information on local wildlife, and there is a deer museum nearby.

Continue along the single-track road through Glen Torridon, signed Kinlochewe. The great red sandstone peak of Liathach (3456 ft) rises to the left and later the quartzite peaks of Beinn Eighe come into view – all of which are over 3000 ft high. The slopes form part of the 10,000-acre Beinn Eighe Nature Reserve.

At Kinlochewe turn right on to the A832, signed Achnasheen. An ascent is made through Glen Docherty and later the shores of Loch a' Chroisg are passed before reaching the edge of Achnasheen.

Turn right here on to the A890, signed Kyle of Lochalsh. The road crosses open moorland, then passes Lochs Gowan and Sgamhain before widening into a double track through the Achnashellach Forest. It becomes a single-track road again as the drive proceeeds along Glen Carron.

Later join the A896 for the return to Lochcarron.

The Torridon Mountains form a massive backdrop to Loch Torridon

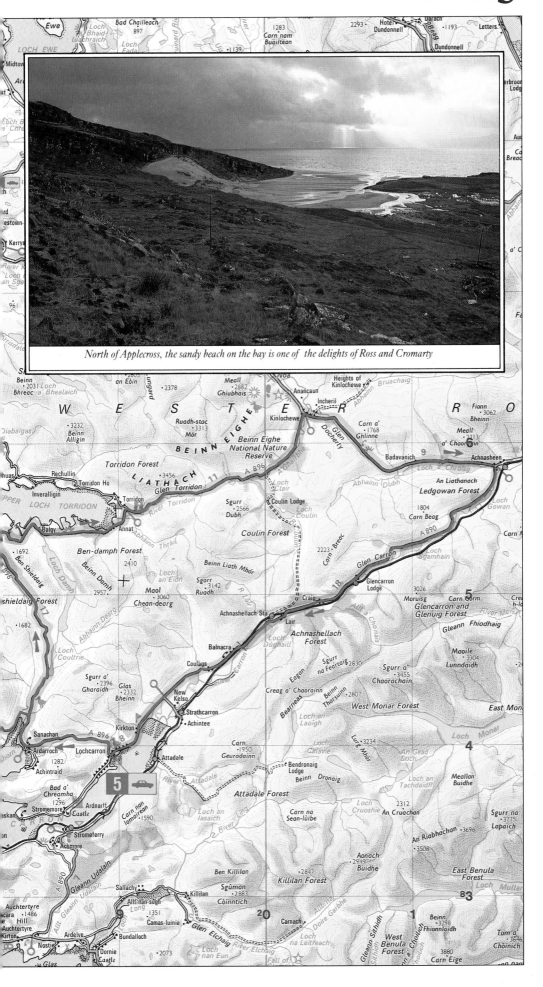

North of Applecross, the sandy beach on the bay is one of the delights of Ross and Cromarty

WALK 1
Tip-top
tour

Allow 1½ hours

John o'Groats may be famed from here to Land's End as the most north-easterly point on the British mainland, but the true owner of that distinction lies some 1¼ miles to the east, Duncansby Head. This easy family walk takes you first to Duncansby Head, then along the cliff-top to a point overlooking the pyramidal Stacks of Duncansby, among the most impressive sea stacks in Britain. The return trip affords superb views of the Pentland Firth and the Orkney islands, as well as nearby Stroma. The edge of the cliff is fenced off at all stages in the walk, and the route is completely safe so long as you keep to the landward side of this fence. The path may become boggy in places, so waterproof footwear is required in all but the driest of weather.

The walk starts at the car park beside the lighthouse (ND404733). Before setting off on the walk it is wise to examine the view indicator in the car park so that the islands and coastal features which will be seen on the return trip can be identified.

Begin by walking towards the lighthouse, and follow the fence-line between the lighthouse and the coastguard lookout. When you reach the coast you are as far north-east and as far from Land's End as it is possible to get on mainland Britain. The lighthouse,

Gannets are often seen offshore from the lighthouse at Duncansby Head

established in 1924, is unusual in having a tapering square tower with a castellated parapet and a movable foghorn. Subject to the keeper's permission, visits to the lighthouse (at prescribed times) are possible. Gannets may often be seen offshore from here.

Follow the fence around the coast, which takes you round the edge of a deep inlet, the Geo of Sclaites. A geo is an inlet formed by the collapse of a sea cave, and this one still has a cave at its head. Excellent views of nesting fulmars may be had from the edge of the geo.

As you walk around the edge of the headland, the Stacks of Duncansby are seen at their best. It may also be possible to see one of the platforms on the Beatrice oilfield from here. Continue up the hill until a fence prevents further progress. The stacks seem quite close from here, and the bedded structure of the old red sandstone is well displayed.

Return to the car park by the same route. There are magnificent views of the Pentland Firth on the way back.

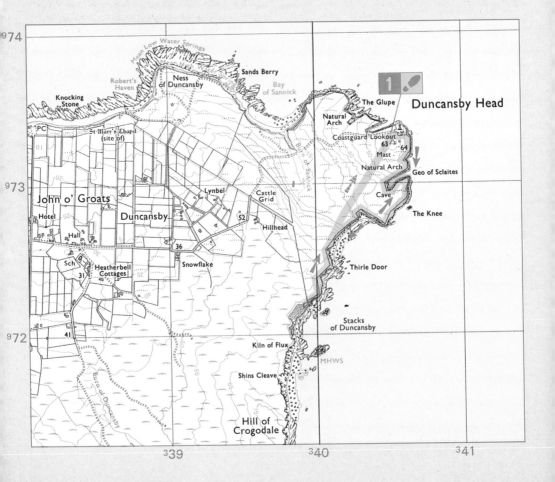

Watch the birdies

Allow 1½ hours

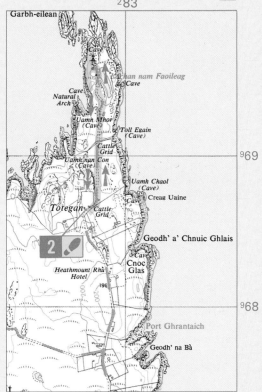

This peninsula juts far out to sea, and is set in a coastline of varied geology and landform. A short, easy walk takes you to the Strathy Point lighthouse; beyond it is a cliff-top rich in plant life which provides one of the best vantage points on the northern mainland for watching passing seabirds. The cliff edges here are treacherous and unfenced, and it is important to stay well back from the cliff slope, especially in high winds.

Begin from the car park at the end of the public road (NC827687). The road beyond this point is private, owned by the Northern Lighthouse Board. Leaving the gate as you found it, walk along the road towards the lighthouse, passing Loch nam Faoileag, the Loch of the Seagulls. Do not enter the precincts of the lighthouse, but proceed on to the cliff-top 'green' beyond, taking care to keep away from the edge. Looking northwards out to sea, it is usually possible to view a range of seabirds flying from east to west and vice-versa. Bird-watching can be spectacular at migration times, when, in addition to the normal inshore seabirds such as fulmar, shag, gulls, guillemots, razorbills and even puffins and gannets, there are Manx shearwaters and skuas.

The cliff-tops around here are noted for their plants, including spring squill, a range of orchids, and the beautiful *primula scotica*, a primrose of a pinkish-purple hue which grows only in Sutherland, Caithness and Orkney. These plants should not, of course, be picked; this is particularly important in the case of the primrose. It is interesting to note that the soils near the cliff are subjected to erosion by wind-blown sea-spray, and that some of the hollows on the cliff-top

receive so much sea-spray that they support plants usually associated with saltmarshes.

Before returning, there is the option of walking to the cliff-top west of the road. The view displays the effects of marine erosion on the complex geology: there are numerous inlets, sea-stacks and caves, as well as a natural arch (NC826694).

The return route should be the same as the outward one, as any attempt to return to the car park any other way would involve climbing fences, and could be very dangerous near cliff-edges.

From the cliff top, there are spectacular views of Strathy Point

| 0 | 200 | 400 | 600 | 800 | 1 | | 2 | | 3 | Kilometres |

| 0 | 200 | 400 | 600 | 800 | 1000 | | | 1 | | | 2 | Miles |

SCALE 1:25000

WALK 3
Tame that dune

Allow 3½ hours

A visit to an old churchyard is followed by a walk along one of the most beautiful beaches on the Scottish mainland, on to a headland where the desert-like sand dunes are so mobile that the road has to be bulldozed clear regularly. Fine views of coastal scenery and birds may be obtained at many points in the walk, culminating in the superb vistas available from Faraid Head. This is not an easy walk for children, however.

Start from the car park at Balnakeil (NC391686).
Balnakeil House, on the right, was built by Lord Reay, chief of the Clan Mackay, in 1774, on the site of an older building which at one time belonged to the Bishop of Caithness. Balnakeil House is now a private dwelling.

Enter the churchyard on the west side of the car park.
A conspicuous granite obelisk with inscriptions in Gaelic, English, Latin and Greek, marks the grave of the famous Gaelic bard Robb Donn (Robert Calder Mackay), while the wall of the church itself, which gives the settlement its name – Baile-na-Cille – the Township of the Church, has the grave of a less illustrious native of the area within its wall. Donald McMurcho (or Macleod) killed at least 18 men for his clan chief, allegedly by throwing them down the Falls of Smoo (NC419670), some two miles to the east. He is said to have demanded to be buried in this position so that a witch who had predicted that she would dance on his grave would be unable to do so. It is more likely, however, that the church officials, conscious of their chief's desire for his retainer to be buried in the church, and also of their own religious duty, resolved their dilemma by burying him half-in, half-out, of the holy building. The inscription of the heraldic panel decorating his grave means: 'Donald McMurcho here lies low. Was ill to his friend, worse to his foe, true to his master in prosperity and woe 1623'.

From the churchyard, walk northwards along the sands of Balnakeil Bay. The strandline usually contains an interesting range of natural and man-made objects. The southernmost part of the beach seems to collect flotsam, and often has a heap of smelly, decaying seaweed up to 3ft high, which is best avoided!

Ringed plovers, oystercatchers and gulls are usually present on the tidal sands, while red-breasted mergansers, shags, eiders and black guillemots may be seen just offshore.

When you reach the northern end of the beach, continue northwards along the road (a continuation of a track along the beach). This takes you up over An Fharaid. The combined effects of rabbits and wind have created a sandy 'desert' here, where even marram, the grass which usually stabilises mobile sand, has been unable to get a grip in the drifting sand. If the wind is strong, this part of the walk will involve getting stung by blown sand. Even where the road is completely covered with sand it is easy to follow its route.

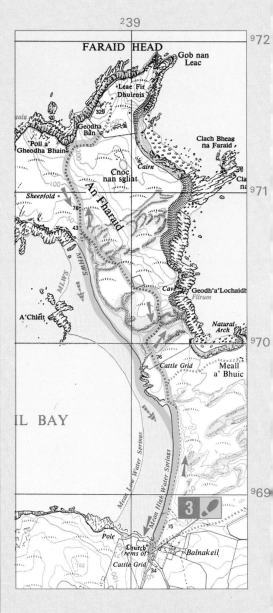

Once through the main blowout area, continue along the track, passing to the left of the enclosure. This takes you through an area of relatively stable dunes and out on to the close-grazed pasture of Faraid Head. Continue on until you reach the fence of the Ministry of Defence installation; this is the limit of the walk.
There are fine views from the left of the road to the west and east, and cliff-nesting seabirds which can be seen here include razorbill, rock pipit and the inevitable fulmar.

Return by retracing your steps until you reach the beginning of the northern beach (NC386707). If the tide is very far out, and still going out, it should be possible to take a short-cut over the beach around the headland. Under no circumstances should this be attempted if you are in any doubt as to whether or not it is safe. *If you decide not to go around the seaward side of the headland, do not go along the beach, but use the track as before: the climb back up to the dunes at the south end would add to the already serious erosion there.*

When you get over (or round) the ridge of An Fharaid, the car park will be in full view, and the route back is straightforward. Do not be tempted to go over the dunes which back Balnakeil Bay: there are serious erosion problems on the dune front, and the areas behind the dunes are used by Balnakeil Farm for grazing its stock.

Reserve judgement

At the last count, Handa had 4000 fulmars

Allow 2–3 hours (depending on the boatman)

Handa is a nature reserve and bird sanctuary off the west coast near Scourie and the circular walk of the island, while easy enough, has some dramatic and unforgettable scenery and wildlife. It is reached by a small ferry from the hamlet of Tarbet, which lies at the end of a side road off the A849 Scourie to Laxford Bridge road.

Park by the jetty (NC164488). The boat which takes visitors across the Sound to land on a sandy bay, will sail only if the weather is suitable and does not run on Sundays. The island is open only in the summer months: for details telephone Scourie 2156 or 2126

The RSPB warden may meet the boat, failing which, walk to the landing spot where there is a hut with information, displays and trail leaflets. Take the path anti-clockwise and keep to the marked circular track to prevent disturbing the bird life. The path takes in all the best of the island anyway and aggressive birds like the bonxies (great skuas) which will normally dive at humans are quite happy to be seen at close range from the path (a moral here, perhaps).

As you walk up the island, pass the sad ruins of the village. Handa is now uninhabited but in 1845 twelve families lived there, ruled (as St Kilda was) by a 'queen' and 'parliament'. Potatoes, fish and seafowl were eaten but the potato famine forced the islanders to emigrate to America in 1848.

Much of the interior is boggy but duckboards have been laid where needed, so ordinary footwear is suitable. The island – and the path – rise steadily and as the north side is reached its big cliffs are suddenly revealed

in dramatic fashion. In the season they are stacked with birds, nesting in their thousands, a sight and sound, of fascinating wonder.

The path follows westwards along the cliffs and in the mouth of one geo (inlet or bay) stands The Great Stack of Handa. This is a monolithic red tower of rock, pierced through by the sea at the base, which rises for some hundreds of feet with every ledge occupied by razorbills (12,000), guillemots (60,000), kittiwakes (14,000), fulmars (4000) and puffins (800). (Figures are island population but you feel they are all here). The Stack was first climbed by man in 1876 by walking a rope out so that it draped over the top, then others of the party swarmed along it, an escapade repeated only once in modern times.

The path then climbs to Sithean Mor (The Fairies' Big Hill). At 403ft, this is the Island's summit, with extensive views down the coast to the Old Man of Stoer and the mountains of Quinag, Suilven and Assynt. To the east the fang of Ben Stack rises over the scoured wastes. Divers call on the lochans and there is bedlam on the cliffs.

As you walk on, the path loses height but the interest remains. Shag sit on the rocks of the SW corner and otters or seals or even whales may be spotted. However long the time agreed with the boatman, it will prove quite inadequate; one visit to Handa Island is not enough.

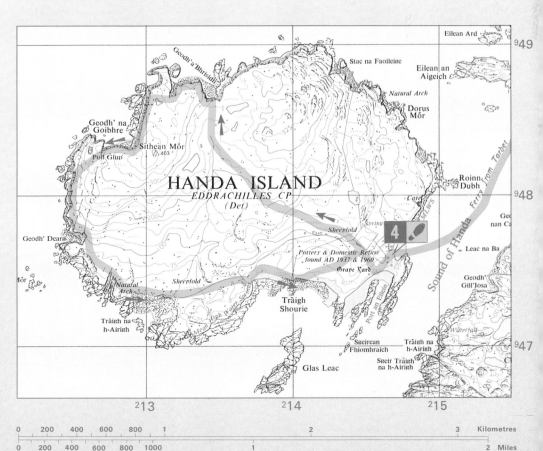

SCALE 1:25000

WALK 5
Wildlife
Ferryland

Allow 3 hours

This walk takes you over a relatively stable dune system, then through a pinewood. The area is very rich in wildlife, and is a nature reserve run by the Scottish Wildlife Trust.

The car park at Littleferry (NH806957) is the starting point for this walk, and is reached by driving south as far as the buildings and turning left. The gravel pit some 250 yards to the north is not a car park. The dunes are locally very susceptible to erosion, and cars must *not* be taken beyond the car park.

Begin the walk by going back to the road and turning left. This brings you to the hamlet of Littleferry, which was formerly an important port for East Sutherland, as well as the main route across Loch Fleet before the Mound Embankment was built in 1816.

Walk back to the car park and take the path out to the right. Continue along the coast until you reach the point (NH813956). This takes you over a series of shingle ridges which were formed during a period of changing sea levels which followed the end of the last glaciation. Along this route there are superb views of Coul Links, the more mobile dune system on the other side of the channel. The flow through this channel can be spectacular. There are always eiders and oystercatchers around here; in winter wigeon and long-tailed duck may be seen. This site is also famous for its resident king eider (which is not always visible, alas).

From here proceed northwards to 'Palm Beach'. Here a small group of planted pines is all that remains of a much larger clump which began to succumb to marine erosion in the late 1970s. Evidence of a dune breach may also be seen here, and a flat, low-lying area is often flooded by the sea in winter. In addition to the usual marram grass on the dune front here, there is also the broad-bladed sea lyme grass. The drier inland parts of the dunes are dominated by heaths and lichens.Skylarks breed on the dunes, and a range of common butterflies may be seen on warm summer days.

Continue northwards until you reach the go-kart track. Bear left of the track's boundary fence, and turn left when you reach the access road. As you cross Golspie golf course, be sure to give way to golfers.

On reaching the Littleferry road, turn left and walk southwards towards Littleferry, through the pines, until you come to a large lay-by on the right, where there is a notice proclaiming the presence of the nature reserve. Climb the stile and take the path through the trees to the west. These Scots pines were planted at the turn of the century, after a native pinewood had been clear-felled.

From here, take the path which leads off to the left, taking you south along the east bank of the stream (the side nearest the road).

On reaching the sands, turn left and climb back up to the road. The view inland from here is superb, and waders and wildfowl may be seen feeding on the invertebrates in the sand.

On regaining the road, turn right and walk southwards until you get back to the car park.

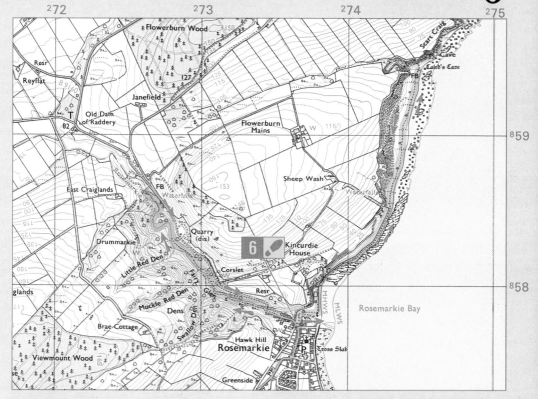

Children's favourites

Allow 45 minutes and 1 hour respectively

This walk is in two parts, with a common starting point at the burnside car park beside the A832. This is at the northern end of Rosemarkie village near the Plough Inn. Both walks have a special attraction for children.

The Fairy Glen has a secretive elfin quality which will appeal to imaginations both young and old. This is a pleasant walk for all the family.

From the car park (NH736578), turn right and walk about 80ft towards the roadbridge and signpost for the Fairy Glen. After 90ft, fork right along a network of shady streamside paths (take care on the small bridges made of tree trunks) under tall hardwood trees. These culminate in two dramatic waterfalls, the final one forming the centre-piece in a natural bowl-shaped amphitheatre.

From here you can either climb out of the glen by a path on its right bank and return by the main road or, preferably, retrace your steps to the car park.

The second walk along the Rosemarkie Coast has the irresistible combination of sand, rockpools, a cave and swing-park.

From the same car park, walk downstream to the Plough Inn and cross the water by a small footbridge, then alongside the football pitch to the shore. By the bridge, a soft sandstone cliff high on your left is an indicator of the spectacular erosion which has led to the formation of the Fairy Glen and given rise to the distinctive red quality of the beach and seashore rocks. The view from the beach across the Moray Firth to Inverness-shire is dominated by both the old and new. The squat grey cubism of Fort George, built to quell the Highlands after the Jacobite Rebellion of 1745, sits incongruously next to the slender cranes of an oil-rig fabrication yard, symbol of a 20th-century upturn in the Highland economy.

Subject to the tide, one may either walk on the sand or along a grassy path. To take the path, first climb the stairs at the end of the concrete frontal path. If you choose to walk on the firm sand (it's easier going), avoid being caught in the small bay as the tide comes in, otherwise you will get wet feet. The end of the walk is at Caird's Cave under Scart Crag some 1½ miles north of the village.

Nearby on the A832 is Fortrose Cathedral

A route with a view

Allow 1 hour

The area above Loch Maree offers walks of character among wild and romantic scenery. Some of the routes are not easy, so pity the poor postman who travelled that way every working day of his life. The road you take is a new one and it is all too easy to drive along it at twice the speed of seeing anything. Loch Maree deserves a *walk*.

Loch Maree – a walk among the Highland's most romantic scenery

The woods, which are such a feature of the walks in this area, are remnants of the northern limits of the forest that once covered Scotland. Iron-smelting on the north side of the loch in the early 18th century saw many trees cut down, while north again the country is too harsh even for Scots pines. These pines are majestic and here they are still home to one of Britain's most elusive mammals, the pine marten. If you are lucky you may see one late in the day when it comes to have a rummage in the litter bins.

If steep uphill walking is not your cup of tea, a good draught of Loch Maree's beverage of beauty can be had where the Slattadale Forest Walk has been laid out by the Forestry Commission. Start at the signposted car park and picnic place (NG888721) from where the trail leads, with little uphill-going, to a superb viewing area looking across to the small islands. Loch Maree is dotted with these islets and Isle Maree (from St Maelrubha) has sacred associations going back to Columban times. As late as the 17th century, bulls were sacrificed on Isle Maree where a well supposedly cured insanity. Certainly the loch has a feel of antiquity to it and an alluring quality all its own.

The trail is part of a pre-road track through to Poolewe so you can walk on further, but will have to return the same way.

Tree-lined climb

Allow 2 hours

The site of this walk on the east side of Loch Ness is depicted in a popular 19th-century print as a place of ambush, where claymore-wielding clansmen crouch behind massive boulders ready to surprise an unsuspecting drover and his shaggy herd. The gorge is an ancient glacial meltwater channel and is still susceptible to seismic disturbances associated with the Great Glen fault which is now partly filled by Loch Ness. This is not a walk for the uninitiated or the unfit, and a good pair of walking shoes is recommended.

The walk starts at the Inverfarigaig Forest Centre (NH522237). Turn right on leaving the car park and follow the single-track public road for ¼ mile. Do not follow the forestry signs at this stage. At the roadside a lichened stone commemorates the geologist James Bryce who fell to his death opposite this spot. Further upstream the cleaner boulders of a recent rockfall have, fortunately, been intercepted by the streambed before they could reach the road.

Fork right into Glen Liath, and right again after ½ mile (keep a watchful eye) and on to rising grassy track to meet a forest road. Glen Liath, the 'Grey Glen', is characterised by the massive boulders which litter the bottom. Between these boulders, road and stream pick their routes.

Follow the forest road uphill to Lochan Torr and Tuill (look out for a yellow arrow) and 90 yards beyond the lochan turn left on to a narrow path which climbs steeply to a ridge crest. Handrails assist in the climb. Looking back from this point the Monadhliath mountains ring the horizon and beyond their tops some 20 miles of empty plateau and peat moss play host to deer and eagle before one reaches Aviemore and human habitation again.

Steeply descend the northside of the ridge to reach a gravelled forest road and pass a stockaded log cabin of Treasure Island *design. At the second crossroads turn right and left again at 45 yards to descend to the car park, Forest Centre and your starting point.*

From Inverfarigaig, Loch Ness and the massive Monadhliath Mountains are glimpsed

SCALE 1:25000

Map detail showing Dog Fall, River Affric, Coire Loch and surrounding area with grid references 228, 229, 230 across the top and 829, 828, 827 down the left side.

The hidden lochan

Allow 1½ hours

Fascinating scenery and a lively river form part of this walk, which is about 45 minutes' drive away from Inverness. The first part of the walk is easily managed but later there are some steep climbs which will not suit the inexperienced, elderly or unfit. The more able will find that reaching the lochan is well worth the effort, but stout shoes or boots should be worn.

This walk starts from the Dog Fall car park (NH284283) on the north bank of the river Affric. Follow the riverside path downstream for about 330 yards, then cross the road and continue on a higher level until the path returns to the river gorge and a graceful footbridge which spans it. Cross the river and climb a high stile over the deer fence, then fork right on a narrow path under birch trees. These give way to pines as the path climbs very steeply to meet a forest road.

Strategically placed benches along the walk allow rest for the weary and give an opportunity to view the superb scenery.

Turn left along the forest road and left again at the path signposted for Coire Loch. This path leads you into a secret bowl-shaped hollow with a tiny loch trapped between high ridges and gnarled sentinel pines. Touch and smell these trees, inspect the massive stabbed bark (the fissures are home for a hundred different insects), and examine the delicate lichen structures. These are all the direct descendants of the first plants to colonise this area when the last pocket of ice left its sheltering hollow some 10,000 years ago.

You don't have to be a biologist or an earth scientist to appreciate such a place. Sit down for five minutes on the bench high above the lochan and feel the slightly spookey quality of its stillness.

Continue following the path as it descends steeply to the river bank again. Return to the car park by the roadside, stopping to enjoy views of the gorge from the various viewpoints.

Inverness – capital of the Highlands – is 45 minutes' drive from this idyllic walk

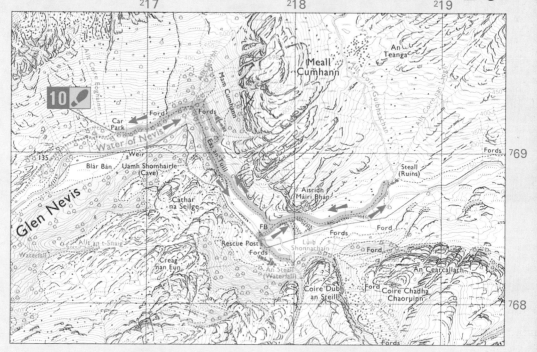

Below Ben Nevis

Allow 2 hours

This classic walk is on clear but stony, rough footpaths which pass through a gorge of Himalayan proportions to visit one of the country's best waterfalls. Stout footwear is advisable and the drops along the path demand caution.

Park at the head of Glen Nevis (NN168691) in a car park beside the famous 'waterslide' which descends 1500ft off Ben Nevis, the highest mountain in Britain. The road up Glen Nevis, from Fort William (where there is an interesting museum), is twisty and narrow with some fine scenery.

Where the road crosses the river at Polldubh, park briefly, because the bridge spans another fall worth seeing. The Polldubh Crags above the road are a popular rock-climbing location; you may well see climbers in action.

From the car park follow the path along into the woody gorge. There is a slightly awkward stream to cross, and later the remains of a 20-year-old rockfall lies on the path. The rubble descends almost to the main river. The gorge narrows and you may notice the carved whorls and curves of water action on the rocks, even 100ft overhead. When the water is in spate, this can be an awesome place. In drier conditions you will notice that the rocks in the river bed have been carved into fantastic shapes by the power of the river – many would make impressive sculptures.

There is a sudden change of atmosphere as you leave the gorge to stroll across a green and placid meadow, beyond which is seen the great Steall Falls, which tumble down from the Mamore Hills in a sweeping veil. A wet day ensures the most

The highest mountain in Britain, Ben Nevis offers up a towering backdrop

spectacular scene so don't be gloomy about it raining.

If you are feeling adventurous you can cross a three-wire suspension bridge to pass the white cottage (a locked climbing hut) and reach the foot of the falls; everyone can wander along the right of way for another quarter of a mile. It is rather muddy at times, but the Steall ruins, beside a river of many little falls, are a point of interest at this charming spot.

The path eastwards doesn't really hit a tarred road again before two or three days of walking so it is best to return from Steall!

At the mouth of the gorge, going back, there is a more energetic alternative path for the fit walker. Turn up the slope by the zig-zags and follow it along and down again. From the highest point the fine view is at its most extensive. This path merges with the outward one to lead back to the car park.

0	200	400	600	800	1		2		3	Kilometres
0	200	400	600	800	1000		1			2 Miles

SCALE 1:25000

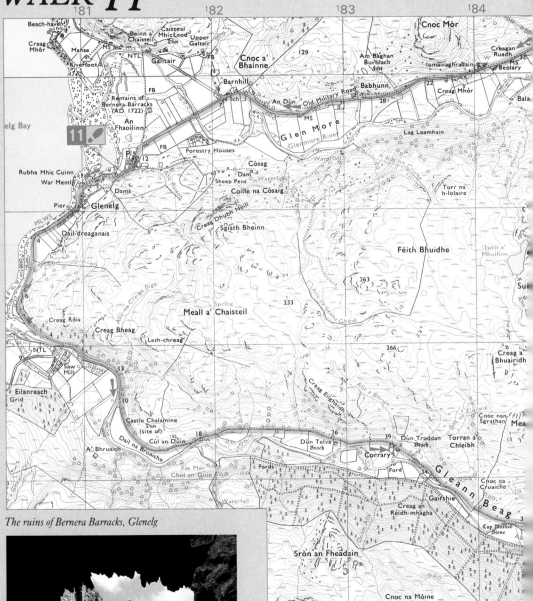

The ruins of Bernera Barracks, Glenelg

The Glens of Glenelg

Allow 5–6 hours (2 hours for a shorter version)

This circuit deserves a leisurely day because there is a good deal to savour. It leads through one of the most pleasant corners in the west and provides a cross-section of Highland history.

Park in Glenelg village (NG813193) near the Telford Inn, named after the great engineer who improved so many miles of Highland roads. Mam Ratagan pass to Glenelg is one of the most spectacular drives in Scotland (there is a viewpoint over Kintail at the summit) and is the route Dr Johnson and Boswell took in 1773. As you enter Glenelg you will see the ruins of the 1722 Bernera Barracks, on the right. North of Glenelg is the Kylerhea ferry to Skye.

Walk on southwards on the Arnisdale road. (This road is worth taking by car, incidentally, for, although it comes to a dead-end after 10 miles, the fjord-like scenery of Loch Hourn is outstanding).

Pass Glenelg's extravagant war memorial and the cottages by the shore before turning off at the first junction to follow up Gleann Beag (The Small Glen), a quiet place of charm. The impressive Eas Mor (Big Fall) will be seen across the valley after half a mile and shortly after that, you will reach the brochs of Dun Telve and Dun Troddan. They are among the best surviving examples of these mysterious and impressive fortifications which are unique to Scotland. There are descriptive notices to help visitors, and enthusiasts will find other prehistoric sites in the glen. The tarmac road ends at Balvraid Farm and the track beyond has a feeling of real wildness to it.

After two miles the lonely lily loch, Loch Iain Mhic Aonghais, appears. From beyond it, the view back is to Ben Sgriol, the finest peak of the area. An even better view is obtained by scrambling up Torr Beag, the bump above the track. This is also a prehistoric fort site.

The path becomes indistinct beyond Torr Beag but cut across to Suardalin Bothy (shelter) – the only visible building – and carry on round the hillside beyond (it may be rather boggy) to reach Glen More (The Big Glen) where the path follows the river-bank down to a bridge. Cross this and turn left to merge with the military road from Mam Ratagan which is followed back to Glenelg and the welcoming Telford Inn. In upper Glen More you will see the cottages and patchwork fields of a small, Gaelic-speaking, crofting community.

If a whole day is not available, drive to the brochs (look out for the Eas Mor) and then walk to Torr Beag and back. This takes about 2 hours.

| 0 | 200 | 400 | 600 | 800 | 1 | | | 2 | | 3 | Kilometres |
| 0 | 200 | 400 | 600 | 800 | 1000 | | 1 | | | 2 | Miles |

SCALE 1:28000

WALK 12

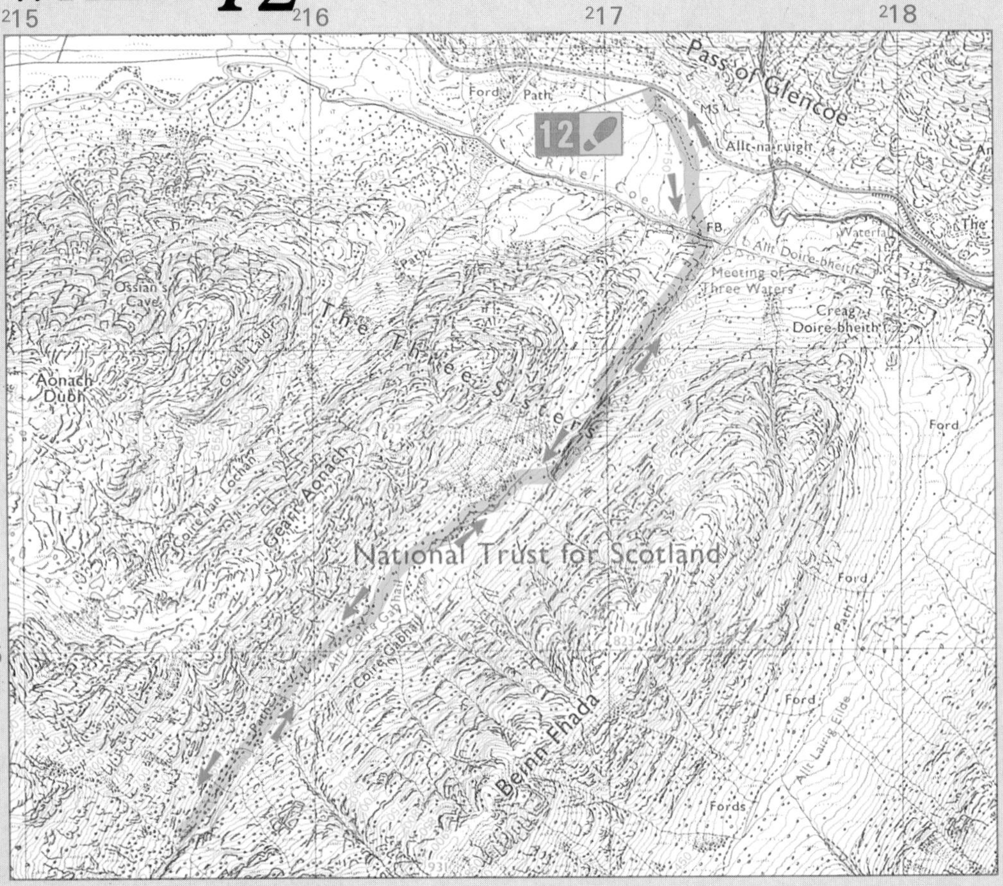

Out of Glencoe

Allow 2 hours

Glencoe is one of the most celebrated spots in Scotland, but The Glen of Weeping (unless the weather is howling) deserves some exploration on foot rather than just a fleeting glimpse as you motor down the glen. Several short sorties are possible, from east to west, as if approaching over Rannoch Moor on the A82, but this is no place for the unfit or inexperienced, and a good pair of walking boots or shoes is recommended as it is fairly slippery in places.

The road sweeps down off the Moor and along under an imposing peak, the Buachaille Etive Mor (the Big Shepherd of Etive) before curving up again to start the Pass of Glencoe itself. Looking left from this rise there is a typical U-shaped glacier valley through the hills. After the road starts to descend more steeply, at The Study, there is an attractive waterfall tucked in a recess, well worth making a brief stop for. A scramble up the knoll on the other side of the road gives a good view of The Three Sisters, as the facing hills are called, and a walk up to Coire Gabhail between them offers the best walk in the glen.

Park in either of the two convenient parking places. The first is about ¼ mile past the solitary cottage of Allt-na-reigh (NN171568) on the righthand side. The other is about ¼ mile further on the lefthand side.

The latter is better for those who don't know the area as the path is better defined. This made path leads down to a secretive footbridge by the Meeting of the Waters and then goes steeply up to a canyon-like passage between the hills. The going is stony and rough in places but you can pick a route to suit your pace and ability. At one time a cataclysmic rockfall piled up boulders in the glacier-gouged valley; these are now overgrown with trees. Even the river has vanished underground, so the place has a strange, silent atmosphere.

Suddenly the character changes and the valley ahead spreads wide, level and green – a cheery oasis surrounded on all sides by dark, rugged mountains, with the river running under glacial deposits. The Gaelic name of this place means Valley of the Booty, and stolen cattle no doubt once knew just how secure it was.

After savouring the spot retrace the route back to the car. On no account wander up on to the peaks. The mountains sweep up on either side as you drive down the glen (one summit is the highest in Argyll) and little imagination is needed to visualise the horror of the winter massacre of 1692. To learn about it, and all aspects of Glencoe, pull off ½ mile beyond Loch Achriochtan, to the popular and well-signposted National Trust for Scotland Visitor Centre. This has picnic tables, a snack bar, toilets, bookshop and numerous displays.

Glencoe is one of the country's most popular climbing areas, but whatever your interests, Glencoe will leave a lasting impression. There is an excellent folk museum in the village by the shores of Loch Leven and the drive round the loch to reach Fort William is a scenic treat.

Monumental viewpoint

Allow 2 hours

Loch Awe, dominated by the ruins of Kilchurn Castle

This is a generally easy (though uphill) walk to a fine 'belvedere', as they used to call such viewpoints. The scene is grand rather than awesome, taking in a sweep of Loch Awe, Cruachan Ben, and many other mountains. Older people may find the gradient tiring.

Park in Dalmally village off the A85 (NN160272). There is ample room at the railway station or at the hotel by the A85 just to the east of the hamlet. From opposite this hotel a loop road leads round by Stronmilchan back to the A85 at Loch Awe, a pleasing diversion. Note the unusual octagonally-shaped church just after you leave the main road here.

Cross the bridge over the railway in Dalmally village and follow this single-track hill road, with its steady gradient, for just over a mile to the obvious monument. –access to which could be rather boggy in some places. This is a superb viewpoint as befits the commemoration of one of the most famous Gaelic poets, Duncan Ban MacIntyre: 'fair Duncan of the songs', as he was called.

MacIntyre lived in the 18th century and, though unable to read or write, composed a volume of work, the very best in Gaelic tradition, comparable with that of Wordsworth in English. (He once gave a 'reading' from his published works and quite unknowingly held the book upside down all through). A great hunter of deer, his verse echoed his love of the hills and the freedom that ended with the aftermath of the 1745 Rising.

Quite a few interesting places can be seen from the monument, so once back at the car these can be followed up.

In the corner of Loch Awe (one of the three largest lochs in Scotland) stands the imposing ruin of Kilchurn Castle, an early home of the Breadalbane Campbells. The ruin fulfills the romantic concept of a 'castle', and a short walk from a roadside car park gives access to it.

The massive hill range beyond the loch is Cruachan, and the deep cleft westwards below it is the Pass of Brander where Robert the Bruce had one of his many narrow escapes in a 14th-century ambush. Set in a hollow in the hills is the Cruachan reservoir, the upper part of an underground pump-storage hydro system (water is pumped up to the reservoir at night when demand is slack and then falls during the day to generate power when most needed). The underground power station is well worth a visit. It is well signposted as you drive along the road to Oban. There are audio-visual displays and you are driven into the heart of the mountain – a fascinating experience.

About half way between castle and power station, on the left, stands St Conan's Kirk, which must not be missed. There is no other church quite like it and, just why, we will leave you to discover. (Its surprises would be spoilt by description).

As you walk back down to Dalmally you are looking over to Glen Orchy and the minor road through it to Bridge of Orchy runs beside some pleasant river scenery.

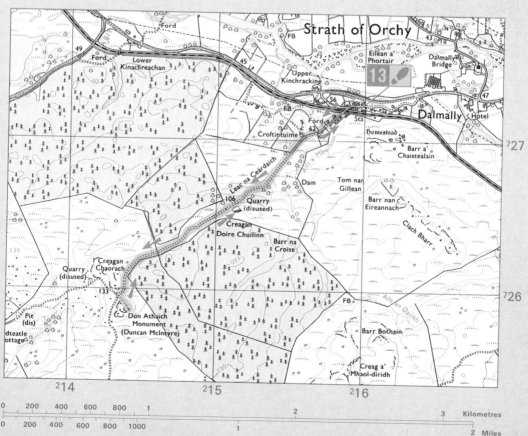

Index

Acknowledgements

The publisher would like to thank the many individuals who helped in the preparation of this book. Special thanks are due to the Scottish Landowners Federation for their advice and guidance.

The Automobile Association also wishes to thank the following photographers, organisations and libraries for their assistance in the compilation of this book. Many of the photographs reproduced are the copyright of the AA Picture Library.

M Adelman 8 Culloden, 9 Kilmorack, 12 Bealach na'Ba, 13 Bein Bhan, 37 Dornad, 40/41 Arddach, 44 Invercrewe, 60 Lochinver, 65 Kinlochleven, 103 Beach, 105 Strathy Point, 109 Fortrose, 114 Bernera; *EA Bowness* 78 Ullapool; *P & G Bowater* 36 Hell's Glen, 65 Perth; *Glenfiddich Distillery* 63; *A Greerley* 22 Skye, 68 Portree, 69 Dunvegan, Kilmuir; *D Hardley* 10 Ben Slioch, 14 Kilchurn, 26/7 Mallaig, 31 Glencoe, 37 Crinan, 41 Museum, 42/3 Glenfinnan, 44 Torridon, 47 Glencoe, 48/9 Glenelg, 49 Inveraray, 51 Loch Hourn, Lochalsh, 52 Kintail, 52/3 Eilean Donan, 54 St. Conans, 54/5 Kilchurn, 55 Lochearnhead, 56 Luss, Inversnaid, 57 Waterfalls, Loch Maree, 60 Torridon Peaks, 74 Balquhidder, 74/5 Arundle, 77 Loch Katrine, 94 Nr. Gairloch; *Highlands & Islands Development Board* 24 Cowal (G. Young), 27 Gairloch (G. Young), 28 Oil Rig, 29 Loch Avon; *S King* 77 Church, 99 Loch Ackray; *The Mansell Collection* Back cover The Grampians, 6 Book of Kells, 8 Culloden, 27 Aberdeen, 37 Highland Chiefs, 73 Highland Clans, 110 Loch Maree, 111 Loch Ness, 112 Inverness, 113 Ben Nevis, 117 Loch Awe; *Nature Photographers* 15 Chequered Skipper (D. Sewell), 18 Red Deer (M.R. Hill), 19 Salmon (C. Palmer), 19 Rose Bay Willow Herb (E.A. Janes), 20 Fulmar (M. Colbeck), 38 Osprey (H. Miles); *R Richard* 46 Dog Falls, 48 Dunrobin, 54 Shin Falls, 73 Strathpeffer, Rogie Falls; *Scottish Tourist Board* 25 Tartan, 61 Haggis, 99 Loch Katrine; *RW Weir* 3 Buchan, 5 Cists Lifts, 7 Blair Atholl, 9 Monument, 21 Pennan, 23 Cruden Bay, 28 Whisky Stills, 32 Aberfeldy, Aberdeen, 33 Arbroath, 34 Falls of Bruar, 23 Pennan, 35 Crathes, Cromrie, 36 Crieff, 38 Dunkeld, 39 Elgin, 40 River Tay, 45 NTS Plaque, Glamis, 46 Glen Cova, 48 Power Lines, 50 Killicrankie, Inverness, 51 Deer Forests, 58 Loch Ness, Castle Urquhart, St. Benedicts, 61 Tarlair, Macduff, 62 St. Cyrus, Mallaig, Drumlithie, 63 Montrose, Glenfiddich, 64 Old Meldrum, 65 Pitlochry, 66 The Queen's View, 67 Glentanner, Balmoral, 70 Loch Morloch, River Spey, 71 Strathspey, Landmark, 72 Dunnottar, Stonehaven, 74 Cairngorm, 75 Tomintoul, Skiing, 78 Whitehills, 79 Queen's View; *H Williams* Cover: Clen Coe, 1 Ben Lawers, 59 Dochart Falls, Ben Lawers, 68 Blackhouse Museum, 76/7 Queen Elizabeth Forest Park, 95 Corriehalloch Gorge, 99 Loch Lomond.

Other Ordnance Survey Maps of the Scottish Highlands
How to get there with the Routemaster and Routeplanner Maps
Reach the Scottish Highlands from Glasgow, Edinburgh, Inverness and Aberdeen using Ordnance Survey Routemaster Map sheets 2 and 4. Alternatively plan your route using the Ordnance Survey Routeplanner Map which covers the whole country and is updated annually.

Exploring with Landranger, Tourist and Outdoor Leisure Maps

Landranger Series
1¼ inches to one mile or 1:50,000 scale

These maps cover the whole of Britain and are good for local motoring and walking. Each contains tourist information such as parking, picnic places and viewpoints, camping and caravan sites.

Sheets 7 to 69 cover the area.

Tourist Maps
These maps cover popular holiday areas and are ideal for discovering the countryside. In addition to normal map detail ancient monuments, camping and caravan sites, parking facilities and viewpoints are marked. Lists of selected places of interest are included on some sheets and others include useful guides.

Explore Ben Nevis and Glen Coe with Tourist Map No 7 and Loch Lomond and the Trossachs with Tourist Map No 9.

Outdoor Leisure Maps
2½ inches to one mile or 1:25,000 scale

These maps for walkers show the popular leisure and recreation areas of Britain. They are packed with detail and include tourist information such as camping and caravan sites, youth hostels, picnic areas and footpaths. There are two Outdoor Leisure Maps for the Scottish Highlands area.

Sheet 8 – The Cuillin & Torridon Hills
Sheet 3 – Aviemore & the Cairngorms (showing Ben Macdui, Braeriach, Cairn Toul and Cairn Gorm)